Praise for the Book

This is a brilliantly written and passionate book which makes a distinctive contribution to African economic ethics. Munyaradzi F. Murove is a trailblazer, taking his readers through sound story-telling and cogent ethical reflections. He refutes romantic descriptions of Africa, highlighting the extent to which greed has set in. Murove challenges popular stereotypes that posit a corruption-ridden Africa and a pristine West. In an informative and challenging way, he exposes the collusion between Western and African greed in bleeding Africa dry. I warmly recommend this book to scholars from diverse disciplines and general readers.

EZRA CHITANDO
Department of Religious Studies, University of Zimbabwe

Presuming that it is not merely the economy that influences values, but also values that influence the economy, Munyaradzi F. Murove explores the ways that greed has affected production and consumption in Africa. He argues that greed has underpinned colonialism, imperialism, finance capitalism and government policies in the post-independence era, and so has been exhibited by not just those of Euro-American descent, but also contemporary African elites. Readers should consider Murove's claim that greed is 'the greatest problem in our human existence'.

THADDEUS METZ
Distinguished Professor, University of Johannesburg

The issue of greed tackled by Munyaradzi F. Murove in this book is not a trivial one. Murove has written this work at an opportune time in the context of global capitalism, with specific reference to its impact on post-colonial Africa. Its novelty lies in that it gives the reader a historical account of modern capitalism from a binary perspective, considering colonial capitalism and political capitalism from an Afrocentric worldview.

In this book, the author asserts that colonial capitalism is not a historical footnote; rather, it continues to manifest itself through modern wars that are being fought with the salient aim of controlling resources. Undoubtedly, the book is very provocative and the topic it tackles has been previously little dealt with. The book will make an interesting read in the market of academic scholarship and lead to further research by students.

HERBERT MOYO
Professor, University of KwaZulu-Natal

GREED

IN POST-COLONIAL AFRICA

GREED

IN POST-COLONIAL AFRICA

THE DEMISE OF COLONIAL CAPITALISM AND THE ASCENDANCY OF POLITICAL CAPITALISM

Munyaradzi Felix Murove

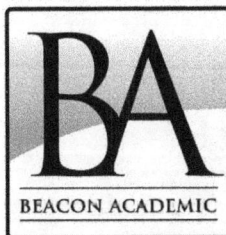

BA

BEACON ACADEMIC

First published in the UK by Beacon Books and Media Ltd
Innospace, Chester Street, Manchester M1 5GD, UK.

First paperback edition published in September 2019

www.beaconbooks.net

ISBN: 978-1-912356-31-7 Paperback
ISBN: 978-1-912356-32-4 Ebook

Cataloging-in-Publication record for this book is available from the British Library

Cover image by Brian Mwamba
Typeset by Siema Rafiq

Contents

Acknowledgements   ix

The Story of Greed in Africa   xi

Chapter 1
The Advent of Modern Capitalism in sub-Saharan Africa   1

Chapter 2
The Main Features of Colonial or Imperial Capitalism   13

Chapter 3
Greed as a Sign of Corrupted Human Nature   59

Chapter 4
The African Mystification of Greed   89

Chapter 5
Greed and the Ascendancy of African Political Capitalism   99

Chapter 6
A Symbiotic Relationship between Corruption and Greed   139

References   163

Index   171

Acknowledgements

This book is a product of my research interests in economic ethics with reference to post-colonial sub-Saharan Africa. It is a result of ideas I gathered during my study and from publications on areas that are closely related to economic ethics in colonial and post-colonial Africa. The writing of the book took place alongside my academic teaching obligations at the University of KwaZulu-Natal. Discussions with colleagues and postgraduate students have informally provided the platform for the book's conceptualisation. I am particular indebted to Professor Emeritus Martin Prozesky for his mentorship and words of encouragement about the primacy of writing in academia. Finally, my appreciation goes to PhD candidate Ms Ethel Chitindingu who provided me with all the technical assistance I have ever needed.

My greatest appreciation is unreservedly due to the editors and publishers of the following journals and books in which some of the ideas expressed in this book were first published: *Persons in Community*, edited by Ronald Nicolson, University of KwaZulu-Natal Press (2008), Springer, *Fairness in International Trade*, edited by Geoff Moore (2010) and the UNISA based *Journal of Religion and Theology* (2008).

The Story of Greed in Africa

Sizwe had worked in the gold mines in South Africa for almost half of his adult life. Unable to read or write, he left his village as a young man in the 1960s in order to marry and pay for the hut and dog tax to the newly established colonial government. For this he needed money, and he had heard that one could only get money as a labourer in the newly found gold fields in South Africa. Full of hope, Sizwe left the comfort of his village community and set out for Johannesburg, the 'city of gold', where stories abound that whoever tried their luck for a better life would never be disappointed. In less than a week, Sizwe was employed in one of the gold mines that mushroomed around Johannesburg. As an underground miner he spent his days digging for gold deep in the belly of the earth, one and a half kilometers beneath the surface.

Whenever he descended into the earth in the automatic electric cage, Sizwe never knew whether he would resurface alive. It felt like death was always lurking behind him like his own shadow and there was an enormous sense of relief when the cage finally landed on the earth. When returning back to their dormitories, the men engaged in story-telling, singing, dancing and beer drinking to help drown the sorrows of the day. Everything they did was in search for that precious metal: gold! All they did was dig further and further and they never knew how much of the precious metal they extracted. The only ones who knew were those white men in suits. In fact, whenever they returned to land, every part of their body was searched by uniformed security guards. Sizwe and his friends, despite risking their lives every day, were never trusted. The same routine took place day after day, month after month, and year after year.

One particular Monday afternoon, Sizwe's friend, Banda, asked him a question that had been bothering him for a long time. Banda wanted to know more about the owner of the mine, who was known to only visit during the annual Christmas party for the mine employees.

"Have you ever seen him? What is he like?" Banda inquired.

Sizwe described the owner, Mr. Cross, as a grey-headed white man in a suit. He said, "My clearest memory of him goes back to one Christmas party many years ago, when he didn't tell us the usual Biblical story about the birth of Jesus. He told us a different story, one that has stayed with me ever since. It went like this:

'Once upon a time, two poor brothers were travelling together on foot for a visit to their relatives. Whilst they were crossing through a valley, they discovered a huge chunk of gold. Both jumped into the air with excitement and jubilation as they knew that their poverty was finally something of the past. However, before they could decide what to do with their newly found fortune, the older brother suggested that the younger brother ought to go buy some drinks so that they could have a small thanksgiving and celebration. The younger brother agreed but whilst on his way, a small voice kept nagging him with an idea that he should poison his brother so that he could have all the gold to himself. If he was to share with his brother, he might end up with less. Indeed, he heeded to that small voice and poisoned his elder brother's favourite drink. However, unbeknown to him, the same small voice had pestered his eldest brother to kill his younger brother with a stone the moment he arrived with the drinks. The older brother lay in wait for the younger brother to arrive and then pounced on him with a stone which killed him instantly. Now the older brother felt satisfied that he had all the gold to himself. But instead of taking the chunk of gold and continuing with his journey, he decided to quench his thirst with the drinks that were brought by his now dead younger brother. After taking those drinks, the poison worked so rapidly that he died on the same spot.'"

"What do you think is the meaning of that story?" Banda asked.

"Perhaps that greed can lead to mutual destruction."

The two men paused. Before Sizwe could say anything further, Banda interjected, "Sizwe, I have heard that Mr. Anglo Cross has been legally forced to give the majority of his business shares to indigenous Africans. The white men came in and wreaked havoc in our country, taking everything that was rightfully ours. But the problem is that the new African owners have concentrated even more on taking the proceeds from those mines without any sense of concern for the majority of their fellow African workers…"

"I have heard such rumours. But who knows what the future will bring?"

Not long after this conversation, Banda and Sizwe returned to their dormitories after work one day to discover that the signage which used to read 'Anglo American Mining Residence' had been changed to 'Mnotho weSizwe (Wealth of the Nation) Mining Residence'. When they inquired about this change, they were told that the ownership of the mine had been changed from Mr. Cross to an African indigenous consortium. Banda and Sizwe were stunned. The hostel was soon buzzing with talk of the greed and corruption that was rife amongst African capitalists.

"Who can blame them when this was the same type of behaviour that was displayed by Mr. Cross's ancestors when they set foot in Africa?" asked Banda. "Maybe they are not so bad, as at least they are of our own."

To this, Sizwe gave a simple reply. "Greed remains abominable regardless of the colour of the person—it remains a devious emotion that is ingrained in human nature."

Chapter 1

The Advent of Modern Capitalism in sub-Saharan Africa

Unbeknown to many Africans, the advent of modern capitalism in sub-Saharan Africa carried with it the promise of civilization and the 'good life'. Colonial anthropologists, explorers, missionaries and historians portrayed an Africa that was in dire need of the benefits that go hand in hand with capitalistic economic development. It was on this basis that colonialists mediated modern capitalism to Africa.

Some post-colonial African scholars have argued that colonialists bequeathed a distinct type of capitalism that was previously unknown to Europe. Colonialism was essentially characterised by primitive accumulation and predation as a mode of economics. Indeed, European countries that had colonial protectorates were mostly interested in extracting resources and cheap labour from Africa for the metropolis. It is no coincidence that most of sub-Saharan Africa was colonised at a time when Europe was in the midst of industrialisation. This meant that Africa was not only a source of raw materials for the colonisers, but also served as a place for expanding the European markets for various commodities. Indeed, the current state of fragility, dependency and under-development of the African nation states is largely a result of colonialism. A number of colonial legislations not only legitimised resource extractions from the colonies, but also gave the colonisers an unfair economic advantage at the detriment of the indigenous people. This is not surprising as the economic logic of colonialism is based on the sole objective of extracting natural resources from the continent. This was epitomised by the manner in which colonialists set about to establish businesses, which were mainly linked to the extraction of natural resources such as raw minerals from the continent, in addition to levying taxes on the majority of African citizens. These scholars also suggest that modern capitalism was introduced without modern capitalist qualities such as thrift, hard work and frugality, as is emphasised in the Weberian spirit of capitalism of the Protestant ethic. Max Weber provides us with long excerpts of the main elements of the Protestant ethic and the spirit of capitalism as follows:

> "Remember, that time is money. He that can earn ten shillings a day by his labour, and goes abroad, or sits idle, one half of that day, though he spends but sixpence during his diversion or idleness, ought not to reckon that the only expense; he has really spent, or rather thrown away, five shillings besides. Remember, that credit is money. If a man lets his money lie in my hands after it is due, he gives me the interest, or so much as I can make of it during that time. Remember, that money is of the prolific, generating nature. Money can beget money, and its offspring can beget more, and so on. Remember this saying, 'The good pay-master is lord of another man's purse.' He that is known to pay punctually and exactly to the time he promises, may at any time, and on any occasion, raise all the money his friends can spare. Never keep borrowed money an hour beyond the time you promised, lest disappointment shut up your friend's purse for ever. The most trifling actions that affect a man's credit are to be regarded. The sound of your hammer at five in the morning, or eight at night, heard by a creditor, makes him wait easily for six months longer, but if he sees you at a billiard-table, or hears your voice

at a tavern, when you should be at work, he sends for his money
the next day; demands it..." (Weber 1958:48–49)

According to Weber (1958:52), these attitudes in business dealings were the causal factors of the ascendancy of modern capitalism. He says, "The concept spirit of capitalism is here used in this specific sense, it is the spirit of modern capitalism. For that we are here dealing only with Western European and American capitalism." He went on to assert that whilst "capitalism existed in China, India, Babylon, in the classic world and in the Middle Ages, this particular ethos was lacking." It can be deduced from the above assertion that for Weber, modern capitalism did not exist in Africa.

The goal of business activities was simply to make more money. However, to be able to make more money, a kind of discipline which could only be found in the Protestant ethic was required. He writes:

> "In fact, the summmum bonum of this ethic, the earning of more
> and more money, combined with the strict avoidance of all spon-
> taneous enjoyment of life, is above all completely devoid of any
> eudaemonistic, not to say hedonistic, admixture. Man is dom-
> inated by the making of money, by acquisition as the ultimate
> purpose of his life." (Weber 1958:53)

But Weber's attribution of the ascendancy of modern capitalism to the Protestant ethic should not be understood to imply that all Protestants had an ethic that was conducive to the ascendancy of modern capitalism. Rather, Weber was referring to the Puritans. The evangelization of Africa during colonialism was mainly carried out by the mainline churches whose attitude towards greed and immense accumulation of wealth was overwhelmingly influenced by medieval Christianity and the teachings of the Church Fathers. As such, one finds many scholars maintaining that the economic approach that dominated medieval Christianity, as found in the traditional economic ethic of the Church Fathers, was not conducive to the ascendancy of modern capitalism in post-colonial Africa (Kennedy 1988:140).

In medieval Christianity, some terms were frequently used in the teachings of the Church Fathers to characterise greed in economic affairs as a manifestation of sin and the dominance of the devil in human lives. For example, avarice, usury and evil are some of the popular terms that were used to describe greed in economic relations. St. Augustine of Hippo propounded that, "Avarice is not a fault inherent in gold, but in the man who inherently loves gold, to the detriment of justice, which ought to be held in incomparably higher regard than gold" (See Gonzalez 1990:215). Evidently, the implication of such a teaching is that material possessions should not be loved in a way that surpasses one's love for human beings.

Equally, the pretence to love God or fellow human beings when done as a means for the attainment of material possessions is a type of behaviour that equates to doing evil. For this reason, St. Augustine described people with excessive love for wealth as "those perverse creatures who would enjoy money and use God, not spending money for God's sake, but worshipping God for money's sake" (See Gonzalez 1990:216). Such a teaching cannot be seen as outdated, as we shall see later on. In the modern age, there has been a phenomenal rise in churches whose practices are at odds with traditional or orthodox churches. These institutions are usually led by charismatic leaders who perform miracles and deliver an evangelical message about worshipping the God of Providence and prosperity. In many Pentecostal churches, divine encounter ensues in the 'miraculous' attainment of wealth in a way that is usually described by the convert as unprecedented in his or her life. This type of Christianity corresponds very well with the type of individualism that is lauded by modern and neoliberal capitalism, in the sense that the individual and his or her material desires are given precedence over the common good of society.

Contrary to the gospel that attaches Providence to prosperity, and divine encounter that supposedly ensues in the over-accumulation of

4

wealth, the economic teachings of the Church Fathers were wholly weaved around the idea of equal distribution of wealth as a practice indispensable to an authentic glorification of God. This school of thought upheld the view that profits accrued from one's economic endeavours could only be justified when shared with the poor. Profits that were accrued with the aim of accumulating more wealth were condemned in the sense that the presence of such profits should be understood as superfluous wealth, the existence of which inevitably leads to usury. Someone who dominated people's economic activities with the aim of taking advantage of their future necessities was committing the sin of usury (Tawney 1926:48–50; Viner 1978:85–90). St. Augustine unambiguously denounced usury when he said: "Not to give to the needy what is superfluous is akin to fraud" and "from those that God gave you, take that which you need, but the rest, which to you are superfluous, are necessary to others. The superfluous goods of the rich are necessary to the poor, and when you possess the superfluous you possess what is not yours" (See Gonzalez 1990:216). The existence of the passion of greed inhibited one from giving that which was superfluous to the needy. Having some goods in superfluity was thus akin to defrauding the poor.

Moreover, the Church Fathers' recommendation of almsgiving from the rich was an exercise in self-redemption from greed. For the Church Fathers, the ideal type of social existence was that which was based on the pursuit of the common good (Viner 1978:20–21). The same type of economic ethic was also upheld by St. Thomas Aquinas who held the Aristotelian view that human economic activities are concerned with "household management" where orderliness is the ultimate purpose (See Schumpeter 1986:91–93; Bigongiari 1973:154). However, in this household management a principle of equity is to be applied. For Aquinas, the principle of equity in household management is something that we can take for granted under natural law, but under human law, it is imperative that the ruler is directly involved in ensuring that that which is superfluous is given to the poor because, as he states, "an injury is done to the poor in not dispensing the superfluous" (Aquinas 1975:229).

In the same vein as the economic ethic of the Church Fathers, Martin Luther launched a scathing attack on greed in one of his sermons on greed and usury. For example, he introduces his work *On Trading and Usury* as mainly concerned with "financial evils" so that some "people—however few they are—may be delivered from the gaping jaws of avarice" (Luther 1962:245). What horrified Luther was the predominance of greed in the business dealings of business people and merchants. Luther highlights this issue vividly:

> *"When once the rogue's eye and greedy belly of a merchant find that the people must have their wares, or that the buyer is poor and needs them, he takes advantage of him and raises the price. He considers not the goods, or what his own efforts and risk have deserved, but only the other man's want and need. Because of his avarice, therefore, the goods must be priced as much higher as the greater need of other fellows will allow, so that the neighbour's need becomes as it were the measure of the goods' worth and value." (Luther 1962:248)*

In the above excerpt from Luther's sermon, it is evident that greed and usury are words that can be used interchangeably as in the economic ethic of the Church Fathers. Ernst Troeltsch does not overemphasise when he says that in Luther's economic ethics, "the continuation of the patristic and medieval prohibition of usury is taken for granted, because profits accrued in one's business activities were supposed to be 'paid back' to the community" (Troeltsch 1931:556). However, some scholars have maintained that this patristic economic ethic inherited by mainline churches was inhibitive to the ascendancy of the spirit of modern capitalism, which thrived mainly on greed.

However, the motif of equating economic success to God's favour was later developed by the Puritans (or reformed Protestants) where it became part of the rationale of modern capitalism as a distinct economic system. In this way, reformed Protestantism helped people to see capitalistic economic activities in a more positive light. This differed sharply with the previously held image of a capitalist as someone whose soul was wholly tainted by the sin of avarice. Reformed Protestantism is thus considered to have opposed this orthodox medieval economic teaching by insisting that capitalistic business activities should be appreciated as a calling like all other divine callings. It is this brand of Protestantism which Max Weber identified as a stimulant to the rise of the spirit of modern capitalism in North America and Europe. For the Puritans, one's economic activities were simply an obedient service to a divine calling which was supposed to be accompanied by qualities such as frugality, thrift, discipline and hard work (Troetsch 1931:557; Hill 1958:226; McGrath 1988:222).

Other scholars such as Richard Tawney do not wholly agree with Weber's thesis. For example, Tawney argued that before the ascendancy of Protestantism, the Catholic Church was involved in usury through the selling of indulgences and the undertaking of colonial economic expeditions. He claims, "[The] Reformation released forces which were to act as a solvent of the traditional attitude of religious thought to social economic issues, it did so without design, and against the intention of most reformers" (Tawney 1926:94). However, Weber and Tawney do concur on the idea that the Puritans taught an economic ethic of individualism, thrift and frugality that was conducive to the ascendancy of modern capitalism. More specifically, the teaching of reformed Protestantism of the individual as solely accountable to God helped to free the individual from the traditional communal sense of accountability. As Robert Heilbroner wrote, "Acquisitiveness became a recognized virtue—not immediately for one's private enjoyment, but for the greater glory of God" (Heilbroner 1972:33; cf. Bujo 1997:163). Thus, the ascendancy of modern capitalism required a severely individualistic understanding of a person as a divinely created egoist. As for the reformed Puritans, greed in one's economic activities became part and parcel of divine calling. The way business operated became something that was in accordance with the laws of God. A Puritan by the name of Heinrich Gossen preached that the pursuit of self-interest in business activities ought to be considered something that is in accordance with the plan of God. Gossen urged, "Organize your actions for your own benefit. God implanted self-interest in the human breast as the motive force for progress. By following self-interest, we follow God's will. Going against self-interest only inhibits God's plan. How can a creature be so arrogant as to want to frustrate totally or partially the purpose of his creator?" (See Daly and Cobb 1989:89).

Assuming that Weber's thesis was true in claiming that the Protestant ethic was responsible for the ascendancy of modern capitalism in Europe and North America, is it possible that in some social context where this ethic was not prevalent, modern capitalism failed to set its roots successfully? The advent of colonial capitalism in Africa was based on the ethic of unbridled exploitation, coupled with acquisitiveness and marginalisation of Africans from governance and decision-making. Indeed, colonialism was not only predicated on notions of white superiority juxtaposed with black inferiority, but it was also based on the insatiable appetite of colonisers to control and extract the continent's vast natural resources.

The story of Sizwe and Banda which was narrated at the beginning is a story of the advent of capitalism in Africa, where greed remains the salient metanarrative of human economic relations in both colonial and post-colonial Africa. Under colonialism, white people put systems in place that enabled them not only to control the vast empires in the colonial state but also to possess unbridled wealth which no one could historically account for. Gold and diamond mines have been operational for decades and some for over a century, but it is difficult to account with certainty how much was extracted and where these minerals went. Indeed, no one person or institution can claim to have the ability to give an accurate account of where those minerals were taken. Since most of the companies that were involved in the mining of these minerals had some connections with the colonising country, the only plausible explanation is that most of the mineral wealth had been expropriated and expatriated to the colonial country or the imperial power. Thus, some scholars have pragmatically suggested that colonialism was not about spreading the goods of capitalistic development to the colonised countries; rather, it was a competition in expropriation and expatriation of the resources from the colonised African nations.

Services such as education and healthcare were provided to the majority of the African populace for instrumental reasons, i.e. with the aim of facilitating the colonial process of expropriating and expatriating the resources from the colonised in the newly established mines, companies and farms. Indeed, colonial education was designed to give Africans critical skills that would enable them to become more docile and become effective vehicles for the predatory and accumulative nature of modern capitalism. Native education in much of colonial Africa was focused on ensuring that Africans acquired skills such as literacy and numeracy to enable them to undertake clerical duties that would make the administration of the colony much easier. An example of this comes from a text that was intended to teach children about hygiene in Benin: "The white people need palm-oil, but the palm tree does not grow in their cold home country. They need cotton, maize and other things. If you die, who will then climb up the palm tree, who will produce the oil, who will carry it to the company?" (See Bujo 1998:189). In this way, colonialism introduced capitalism to Africa in pursuit of the economic interest or greed of the colonisers.

The Resemblance between the African Traditional Economic Ethic and Medieval Economic Ethic

An argument has been proffered by other scholars which gives the impression that African traditional collectivistic or communitarian values were wholly commensurate with the economic ethic of the Patristic era. Jomo Kenyatta echoed this when he said, "The selfish or self-regarding man has no name of reputation in the Gikuyu community. Religious sanctions work against him, too, for Gikuyu religion is always on the side of solidarity" (Kenyatta 1953:119). In other words, economic activities are expected to promote the common good. Thus, in this regard, greed was tempered with the prestige motive that manifested itself in sharing one's wealth with other members of the community. The underlying presumption was that communal harmony and tranquillity could only prevail when wealth is collectively enjoyed (Murove 2008:94; Gelfand 1981:15; Bujo 1998:162).

The African traditional attitude towards wealth blatantly contradicted Max Weber's Protestant ethic, which he claimed was characterised by business qualities such as hard work and frugality. This observation was succinctly put by Benezet Bujo when he said that in traditional African societies, "Avarice was one of the most detestable vices. Hence, the border between avarice and frugality is unclear in Africa because saving money, for instance, could be taken as an excuse for refusing to offer necessary assistance to others" (Bujo 1998:163). In other words, African traditional attitudes towards wealth was more oriented towards the promotion of immediate material enjoyment. The advancement of human wellbeing and enjoyment appears to have been the main African traditional attitude towards wealth. In this regard, the idea of accumulating vast amounts of wealth, accompanied by austerity or thriftiness as the indispensable foundation towards further accumulation, remained an unintelligible idea in traditional African economic ethics. Ali Mazrui characterised this traditional African economic ethic as primarily driven by the prestige motive. With the aim of emphasising its primacy, Mazrui said:

> "This prestige motive in traditional [African] societies raises serious economic problems. Because of the communal moral obligations that are put on the prestige motive, earnings are expended on entertainment and hospitality, on ostentatious weddings, expensive funerals and initiation ceremonies. In addition, there is the crippling desire to fulfil obligations towards distant cousins and aunts." (Mazrui 1999:922)

In the prestige motive, there was an ardent belief that the sharing of one's wealth was a goodwill gesture which could be used to indulge the ancestors. Whenever one shared his or her wealth with others, it was believed that such a gesture pleased the ancestors and as a result, one could expect benedictions from the immortals, usually in the form of more wealth. Indeed, a cursory glance at African proverbs demonstrates the salience of the motif of sharing wealth and the subsequent benefits to the larger community. The African political economy was largely characterised by the prominence of the cooperative mode of behaviour in the economy as well as in political decision-making.

Modern capitalism was not mediated through the Weberian Protestant ethic, but through a culture of acquisitiveness and expropriation. Duress and anarchy in the process of acquisition and expropriation of wealth were the norm in the colonial territories. Colonial administrators promulgated laws that were mainly aimed at expropriating land and minerals from the indigenous African people. The colonial culture of acquisition and expropriation of land and minerals left the majority of the African indigenous population in a situation of abject destitution. Moreover, the colonial culture of predatory accumulation created a dynamic that fortified a hierarchy between the colonisers and the natives. Indeed, capitalist penetration of Africa was characterised by domination of the natives, and ultimately resulted in the dependence of African economies on the Western world.

Colonial rule depended on cheap labour in order to effectively extract the continent's natural resources. To this end, the colonial system included a complex set of processes designed to ensure that Africans had limited options except to sell their labour. For example, the critical feature of colonial accumulation included appropriation of land owned by Africans, coupled with the annihilation of African currencies and their subsequent firm replacement with Western currencies. This meant that Africans had to rely on the colonial currency to engage in their day-to-day commercial activities. Once Africans were disposed of their land

and they had no reliable means of production, and as soon as the new colonial medium of exchange was firmly in place, they were forced into wage labour in order to acquire this currency and pay for goods, services and taxes. In fact, the dispossession from land, the monetisation of the African economies, and the insistence of tax payment in currencies introduced by Europeans, cumulatively explains why many Africans such as Sizwe and Banda, whom I mentioned in the story at the beginning, had to make sojourns to the gold mines and work for the 'white man'.

Colonial capitalism defied all the known textbook rules of entrepreneurship. The end of colonialism which was brought through the independence of African states did not, however, emerge with changes in these subservient relationships between the Africans and former colonisers. In fact, what is being argued here is that the end of colonialism still reflected the dominant nature of the relationships between the colonisers and natives. This dominant and predatory relationship has not completely been eradicated from current interactions in post-independent Africa. The legacy of European rule has continued to manifest in the political economy of Africa. What is notable is that primitive accumulation is still a key feature of the post-colonial African state's socio-economic and political reality, through which the current form of modern capitalism was mediated to Africa.

As I explore in this book, post-colonial Africa is dominated by a type of capitalism which I call 'political capitalism'. It is a type of capitalism that is championed by most African politicians as 'indigenization' or 'black economic empowerment', in which emphasis is put on the need to indigenize the means of production to overcome the economic remnants of colonialism. It is sometimes described as 'economic nationalism', implying a deliberate attempt by politicians to make capitalism culturally inclusive by propagating polices that aim to transfer wealth into African hands. Is there a relationship between colonial capitalism and post-colonial political capitalism? This book will leave the reader at liberty to answer this question themselves.

Chapter 2

The Main Features of Colonial or Imperial Capitalism

Colonialism was experienced differently in many parts of the world through a process of ruthless conquest and subjugation of the natives. In the conquered territories where the economic prospects for prosperity were great, colonialism or imperialism was carried out mercilessly and savagely. The end goal of colonialism was to extract the rich and abundant natural resources of the continent and this was to be done by all means necessary, including extralegal. As such, killing of the indigenous populations, slavery, and expropriation of land and minerals from indigenous communities became integral to the ordering of colonial societies. The brutal nature of the colonial system is more salient in the Congo, where more than 8 million people died during the conquest of King Leopold II of Belgium. Africans in Leopold's Congo worked under slave-like conditions and could easily be beaten, whipped, or punished for failing to meet production quotas. Here we encounter an example of anarchy turning into law. Expropriation of mineral resources and land was justified through acts of parliament which ensured that what was promulgated as law was actually a piece of legislation deliberately aimed at depriving the indigenous African people of their right to self-govern and control their own resources. As we shall see later on, the history of expropriation of land and minerals from the indigenous Africans is strongly entrenched, with specific reference to Southern Africa. In this respect, capitalism was not mediated to Africa through Max Weber's Protestant ethic. Weber's description of the economic culture of colonial or imperial capitalism is profound:

> "In general and at all times, imperialist capitalism, especially colonial booty capitalism based on direct force and compulsory labor, has offered by far the greatest opportunities for profit. They have been greater by far than those normally open to industrial enterprises which worked for exports and which oriented themselves to peaceful trade with members of other polities. Therefore, imperialist capitalism has always existed wherever to any relevant degree the polity, or its subdivisions (municipalities), has engaged in a public collective economy for satisfying demands. The stronger such collective economy has been, the more important imperialist capitalism has been." (Weber 2009:168)

Colonial capitalism was thus characterised by Weber as 'booty capitalism', with its main orientation being pure acquisitiveness and the application of unconventional methods to secure natural resources and land. Colonial capitalism was also more profitable than the conventional form of capitalism that operated under the rules of fair trade. It created demands that might not have existed prior to its advent.

Weber went on to say that under colonial capitalism, conquered territories were curved on the basis of their economic importance. In this regard, monopoly of territory was motivated by the pursuit of lucrative looting opportunities, and it is for this reason that Weber made the following observation: "The safest way of guaranteeing these monopolized profit opportunities to the members of one's own polity is to occupy it or at least to subject the foreign political power in the form of a protectorate or some such arrangement. Therefore, this 'imperialist' tendency increasingly displaces the 'pacifist' tendency of expansion, which aims merely at 'freedom of trade'" (Weber 2009:169). Colonial capitalism was not concerned with the promotion of a free market economic system based on the capitalistic principles of free trade and equality before the law; rather, it was based on the principle of total economic control aimed at supporting the economic needs of the colonial metropolitan and the colonial community.

Vladimir Lenin was also among those who saw a symbiotic relationship between imperialism and capitalism, such that these two political and economic systems were inseparable. Lenin asserted:

> *"Capitalism has grown into a world system of colonial oppression and of the financial strangulation of the overwhelming majority of the population of the world by a handful of 'advanced' countries. And this 'booty' is shared between two or three powerful world marauders armed to the teeth (America, Great Britain, Japan), who involve the whole world in their war over the sharing of their booty." (Lenin 1947:13)*

Some of the great wars fought in the history of human existence were thus motivated by a competition among imperialists to loot resources from colonised countries in various parts of the world. One can make the bold assertion that the rise of modern capitalism was at odds with imperialism, whereby military force was used by the powerful capitalist countries to oppressively plunder the resources of weaker populations who fell under the reach of the arm of imperialists.

The acquisition of wealth from the poor populations of the world is described by Lenin as a 'booty' which is shared among the imperialists. According to *The Shorter Oxford English Dictionary*, the word 'booty' means "plunder, or profit acquired in common and so divisible, spoil of war, which [which] is taken by thieves as a prize of war" (Onions 1973:218). This definition implies that booty capitalism or colonial capitalism was based on plundering of resources or wealth in a way that was reminiscent of a situation of war or thievery. In other words, this definition also implies acquiring wealth in a way that is unlawful. As we shall later explore, those who undertook colonial expeditions were usually awarded with vast tracts of lands and minerals that were looted in the conquered territories. Colonialists were more interested in the looting of as much resources as humanly possible in the conquered lands, rather than the spread of free trade in their imperialistic quests.

Nowhere is this story of the instrumentalisation of Christianity more prominent than in the story of King Leopold II of Belgium, who ran the Congo Free State as his personal fiefdom from 1885 to 1908. For example, a letter to the Belgian missionaries by King Leopold II shows that the real intention of evangelizing in the Congo was to plunder its resources for the advancement of Belgian economic interests. For King Leopold, the main task of the missionaries was to evangelize the Congolese in such a way that they viewed the wealth in their own natural resources as undesirable. This assertion is made very clear in King Leopold's own words to the missionaries: "You will go to interpret the gospel in the way it will be the best to protect your interests in that part of the world. For these things, you have to keep watch on disinteresting our savages from the richness that is plenty in their ground to avoid that, they get interested in it [sic], and make your murderous competition and dream one day to overthrow you." Leopold went on to admonish the missionaries by saying, "Your knowledge of the gospel will allow you to find texts ordering, and encouraging your followers to love poverty, like 'Happier are the poor because they will inherit the heaven' and 'It's very difficult for the rich to enter the kingdom of God.' You have to detach from them and make them disrespect everything which gives courage to affront us" (Okoro 2005:1).

The main objective of imperialism was to use all means available—holy or profane—for the looting of material resources. King Leopold II saw the missionary evangelization in Congo as primarily about facilitating the colonial plundering of the resources in the Congo or depriving the Congolese people of their wealth. For him, Christianity had no other purpose besides facilitating the greed of the marauding imperialists by pacifying indigenous Africans on the issue of wealth accumulation. It can be easily discerned from King Leopold II's letter to the missionaries that the main purpose of missionary evangelization in the Congo was about the spiritualisation of the Belgian imperial looting of Congolese resources with a sense of abject disregard of their humanity. This imperial outlook is more nuanced in King Leopold II's letter where he said, "Convert always the blacks by using the whip. Keep their women in the nine months of submission to work freely for us. For them to pay you in sign of recognition—goats, chicken or eggs—every time you visit their villages. And make sure that niggers never become rich. Sing every day that it's impossible for the rich to enter heaven. Make them pay tax each week at Sunday mass" (Okoro 2005:1). The missionary evangelization purpose was thus aimed at fulfilling the objective of looting natural resources from the Congolese.

Critics of colonialism or imperialism have assessed it on the basis that it was primarily dominated by predatory features which were justifiable when one takes into account the human development benefits to be gained by the colonised. Karl Marx believed that the mediation of capitalism through imperialism was a historical fact that was "beneficial to humanity" regardless of the "human suffering it might cause". For this reason, "he regarded the British conquest of India as objectively progressive, since by it the methods of government and production associated with oriental despotism were eradicated and a basis laid for a modern industry" (Cited in Mommsen 1981:30–32). However, for some scholars, imperialism was the by-product of capitalism. This school of thought was adopted by those who regarded themselves as Marxist-Leninist. What has been overlooked in this type of interpretation of colonialism or imperialism is that this historical era brought about a competition in Europe for scarce natural resources, which explorers found to be in abundance in so-called 'savage' territories, such as those that were populated by the Native Americans in America, Aborigines in

Australia and Africans in Africa. The privatisation of natural resources and their scarcity, coupled with a rapid increase in the population of Europe, set the imperial project in motion. With the moral justification of greed in modern capitalism, the European world was no longer capable of supporting its own poor citizens.

Colonial Capitalism and the Spirit of Acquisitiveness and Expropriation

Colonial capitalism was based on an economic system that was mainly acquisitive, with unprecedented expropriation of land and minerals from indigenous African peoples. Under colonialism, African minerals, fertile lands, sacred sites and wildlife sanctuaries were ruthlessly expropriated from the defenceless, indigenous African population for the benefit of individual colonialists without any compensation. Most of these colonial acquisitions were legitimised by laws which made it difficult for indigenous Africans to claim back that which was expropriated from them. For example, what motivated Cecil John Rhodes to invade the lands that were in the interior of the Limpopo River in Southern Africa was not necessarily a nationalistic passion to spread Western civilization through the British imperial aspirations, but his personal belief that there were prospects for the discovery of an abundance of gold that would surpass that which was found in the Transvaal in South Africa.

Rhodes was a colonial capitalist who had an insatiable appetite for wealth. In 1890, he recruited a group of 180 mercenaries who were to accompany him "across the Limpopo River to search for gold and extend the realms of the British Empire." However, he was forced by the British government "to pay for the costs of the column and its accompanying police force out of his own pocket" as well as for all future expenses (Meredith 1979:19). For a period of thirty-three years, what was then known as the 'Rhodesia' territory was given "to a private commercial company, Rhodes' British South Africa Company" (Ibid). Those mercenaries who assisted Rhodes' Pioneer column in the conquest of Zimbabwe were rewarded with the most fertile farmlands of their own choice with a combined acreage of 1,500,000 acres. However, Rhodes' greed was not limited to the expropriation and accumulation of material wealth. He also desired to be recognised as the substitute of the *Mwari* deity (Shona word for God) who was believed to reside at the Matopo Hills, a shrine that is found in Matabeleland. In this way, as well as seizing land from the African indigenous people of Zimbabwe, he also expropriated their religious beliefs.

When the prospect of finding an endless reef of gold proved futile in Zimbabwe, Rhodes and his newly settled white community resorted to farming. The white settler community devised rules and regulations that gave them both political and economic power to pursue the expropriation of land without hindrance from the indigenous African population. According to Martin Meredith, "Legislation was introduced to ensure that African development never posed a serious threat to white interests. Land, jobs and wages were apportioned by race. Within ten years from 1890 nearly 16 million acres were handed out to white farmers regardless of whether Africans were occupying the land or not" (Meredith 1979:21). If we are to recall Weber's characterisation of colonial capitalism, then this type of capitalism can be rendered booty capitalism in the sense that it was based on expropriation and acquisition of wealth under the pretext of self-proclaimed colonial legality. The law was formulated in a way that gave the settler white population the right to complete expropriation of the natural resources of the country at the exclusion of the majority of the indigenous African population. By 1931, through the Land Apportionment Act Rhodesia's 50,000 whites captured 49 million acres of the most fertile land in the country while 1,000,000 Africans had 29 million acres in places that were known as 'Reserves'. Prior to the advent of colonial capitalism, most of these Native Reserves were actually the habitat of wild animals—thus, not suitable for productive human habitation. Such a situation left the indigenous African people without any economically viable livelihoods.

A claim that was used by colonisers as a justification for expropriating the land was that the land was hardly used for economically productive purposes, and that the whole colonial enterprise was aimed at spreading the goods of civilization and Christianity to heathen lands. It is on record that the Boers who settled in Melsetter, Eastern Zimbabwe in 1893 diarized the existence of indigenous African agricultural products such as mealies, rapoko corn, kaffir corn, millet, groundnuts, beans, eggs, fruit, cabbages, sweet potatoes, peas, pumpkins of sorts, watermelons, cucumbers, chilies, tobacco, bananas and lemons (Martin and Johnson 1981:37). In other words, indigenous Africans were involved in agricultural activities before their land was expropriated by European settlers. David Martin and Phyllis Johnson succinctly point out that:

> "...the truth is that when the settlers arrived in 1890 a politically and economically developed system existed. The settlers had mainly come for the gold and over the next twenty years much of their food was supplied by the African economy. When the settlers found there was little gold they turned to farming, in the process destroying the African economic system and forcing the Africans into reserves as they expropriated their land, thereby creating a reservoir of cheap labour for the settler's farms, mines and developing urban centres." (Martin and Johnson 1981:37)

The expropriation of land from the indigenous African people carried with it total deprivation for subsistence living and agricultural knowledge. Without any land, it can be presumed that any agricultural knowledge possessed by the indigenous African people was also expropriated from them. Of all the problems that European rule created in Africa, none had more far-reaching consequences than the illegal and ruthless expropriation of land from Africans, by turning them into slaves for the colonial settlers. Indeed, colonisation paid no regard to the ownership and entitlement that Africans had over their land. The current post-apartheid South African government's proposal of expropriation of land without compensation should be seen as an attempt by the democratically elected government of South Africa to reverse the ills of the imperialistic past, committed by the minority white settler regime. Indeed, the current South African government under President Cyril Ramaphosa seeks to undo the injustices of the land question. In June 1913, the apartheid government of South Africa adopted the 'Natives Land Act', which created a legal framework that effectively disenfranchised blacks from their land, and divided land into the white fertile heartland, juxtaposed with the impoverished black reserves. Effectively, the Natives Land Act resulted in black South Africans becoming impoverished, landless and economically dependent on the white colonial system. After more than 20 years since the official end of apartheid and South Africa's subsequent independence in 1994, this division between the productive core white land and the impoverished and poorly serviced black reserves in South Africa remains at the heart of the continuance of the global economic apartheid. Since 1994, the South African government has struggled to craft a land reform programme to redress the injustices of the 1913 Natives Land Act, and as such, the 'land question' in South Africa has remained unresolved.

Although there have been three waves of expropriation of land without compensation in South Africa, the Natives Land Act, enacted by the British in 1913, was of the greatest significance. This Act was not concerned with returning the land that was previously expropriated from the indigenous South Africans, but the ultimate expropriation of land from the majority of Native South Africans without compensation, in a way that left them completely destitute. This was clearly an act of unreserved self-indulgence. Sol Plaatje's book, *Native Life in South Africa*, clearly outlines colonialist injustices in a way that displays the colonial masters in the same light as the slave masters in the Jim Crow southlands of America. The Natives Land Act turned the colonial settlers into predators against the indigenous African population with whom they stayed as neighbours for decades. The story narrated by Plaatje regarding this Act is painful and extremely traumatising. He illustrates in retrospect:

"*Awaking on Friday morning, June 20, 1913, the South African native found himself, not actually a slave, but a pariah in the land of his birth. The 4,500,000 black South Africans are domiciled as follows: one and three-quarter million in locations and reserves, over half a million within municipalities or in urban areas, and nearly a million as squatters on farms owned by Europeans. The remainder are employed either on the public roads or railway lines, or as servants by European farmers, qualifying, that is, by hard work and saving to start farming on their own account. A squatter in South Africa is a native who owns some livestock and, having no land of his own, hires or farm or grazing and ploughing rights from a landowner, to raise grain for his own use and his stock. Hence, these squatters are hit very hard by an Act which passed both Houses of Parliament during the session of 1913, received the signature of the Governor-General on June 16, and forthwith came into operation.*" *(Plaatje 2007:21–22)*

Essentially, the Natives Land Act was a piece of legislation that was prompted by the greed of the colonial settler community and epitomised their desire to control the vast natural resources of South Africa. As is always the case with greed, this Act was aimed at expropriating land from the indigenous South Africans without compensation. It was enacted with the aim of advancing the economic interests of colonial settlers to the exclusion of the majority of the African populace. Therefore, legislations were enacted with the specific aim of expropriating land and minerals from indigenous Africans. Prior to the enactment of the Natives Land Act, in 1903 the British imperial government set up a South African Native Affairs Commission with the specific aim of devising what they called a 'Native Policy' suitable for South African territories. The commission came up with recommendations, including that "whites and blacks should be kept separate in politics and in land occupation and ownership basis" and that "political power should remain in white hands" (Meredith 2014:510–511). Obviously, such recommendations were aimed at enabling expropriation of land and minerals in favour of

22

the colonial settler communities. It is also common knowledge that the deprivation of political power amongst the indigenous Africans was a powerful mechanism that enabled the economic cake to remain exclusively in the hands of the colonial settler community. Land-grabbing left most of the indigenous Africans destitute to such an extent that they were indirectly forced to rely on white farmers who were favoured by law. As we have seen previously, in the case of South Africa, the consequences of the Natives Land Act were extremely catastrophic to indigenous African people to the extent that they became squatters in their own motherland. Indeed, it was the 1913 colonial South Africa and the Natives Land Act that brought the word 'squatter' into existence. According to Sol Plaatje, "The squatters form a particular section of the community specifically affected by the Land Act, and there is no such person in South Africa as a white squatter" (Plaatje 2007:61). In truth, this 'Natives Land Act' had no other envisaged economic purpose besides expropriation of land from the indigenous Africans.

The word 'squatter' implies someone who does not own a portion of land and occupies land illegally. Being a squatter implies deprivation of land, which is a basic necessity of life. In this way, the Act legalised the colonial greed for land at the expense of the African indigenous people. For example, the Act stated that:

> "Except with the approval of the Governor-General:
>
> A native shall not enter into any agreement or transaction for the purchase, hire, or other acquisition from a person other than a native, of any such land or of any right thereto, interest therein, or servitude thereof, and
>
> A person other than a native shall not enter into any agreement or transaction for the purchase, hire, or other acquisition from a native of any such land or of any right thereto, interest therein, or servitude therefore."

Superficially, this Act sounds altruistic and philanthropic towards indigenous African people but a closer look finds that it was wholly aimed
at expropriating land from the natives to the advantage of the colonial
settler community. Although in reality the indigenous South Africans
were left without any land, the Act itself was crafted in a way that gave
the opposite impression: that the indigenous South Africans were given
land which was protected by the Act from expropriation by the colonial
settler community. This cynicism is more explicit where the Act states:

> "From and after the commencement of this Act, no person oth-
> er than a native shall purchase, or hire in any other manner or
> acquire any land in a scheduled native area or enter into any
> agreement or transaction for the purchase, hire or other acquisi-
> tion, direct or indirect, of any such land or of any right thereto or
> interest therein or servitude thereof, except with the approval of
> the Governor-General." (Plaatje 2007:64)

After the expropriation of land, the land that was left for the majority of the indigenous Africans was in most cases unsuitable for human
habitation and agricultural productivity, and was also complemented by
the stealing of livestock from indigenous African people with impunity.
As Plaatje puts it:

> "The pass law was first instituted to check the movement of
> livestock over sparsely populated areas. In a sense, it was a wise
> provision, in that it served to identify the livestock which one
> happened to be driving along the high road, to prove the bona
> fides of the driver and his title to the stock. Although white men
> steal large droves of horses in Basutoland and sell them in Natal
> or in East Griqualand, they, of course, are not required to carry
> any passes." (Plaatje 2007:84–85)

Indeed, the Natives Land Act cannot be effectively interpreted without
looking at a host of other laws that were passed during the apartheid
system. To solidify their control over land, the colonisers set about to

control the black South Africans' movement and allocate the migration of labour through a series of laws and measures. The pass laws that were enacted in the aftermath of the Natives Land Act partly aimed to rapidly facilitate the expropriation of indigenous South Africans' land and livestock. The natives were not only evicted from their ancestral land without compensation, but were also made destitute and left without any means for survival. The enforcement of the Act and what took place in its aftermath echoes a Zulu idiom that says '*Ukuphuca inkonyana ubisi emlomeni*', literally meaning 'Forcefully taking away the milk which the calf is feeding on for its survival'. Pass laws were designed by the colonial government with the specific aim of disadvantaging the indigenous Africans from having access to the economic cake of the country.

In his tour of the country after the passing of the Natives Land Act by the colonial parliament of Cape Town, Plaatje reported of families who were evicted from their farms after refusing to give the colonial settler farmer their livestock and to work for him. Plaatje's narrative of African lives in the aftermath of the Act shows that greed is intrinsically evil. As he says in his book:

> "It was cold that afternoon as we cycled into the 'Free' State from Transvaal, and towards evening the southern wind rose. A cutting blizzard raged during the night, and native mothers evicted from their homes shivered with their babies by their sides. When we saw on that night the teeth of the little children clattering through the cold, we wondered what these little mites had done that a home should suddenly become to them a thing of the past."
> (Plaatje 1982:89)

The atrocities that were imposed upon the lives of the indigenous African people in the aftermath of the Natives Land Act were so atrocious that they defy comprehension. This piece of legislation can certainly be considered an act that ushered evil upon the indigenous African people, as all their means to subsistence and livelihood were mercilessly decimated through a process of expropriation of land and livestock. Taking into account the historical truism that the Natives Land Act uprooted indigenous South Africans from the soil of their birth, the psychological effects were similarly extremely devastating, especially when one takes into account the fact that indigenous African people historically have a spiritual as well as physical attachment to their land. In traditional thought, the land is spiritually symbolic as the source of identity and common belonging among the living, God, ancestors and the natural environment. Thus, for the South Africans, the expropriation of their land was akin to being stripped of their identity.

However, what the English initiated in the Cape Colony Parliament in the Natives Land Act was later systematically and ideologically implemented by the Afrikaners Nationalist Party in the form of the draconian political system of apartheid. In South Africa, apartheid was a political system that was based on what its adherents called 'separate development' whereby people of Caucasian origin were deliberately privileged. According to Marie Lipton, the main characteristics of apartheid were as follows:

> "(a) The hierarchical ordering of the economic, political and social structures on the basis of race identified by physical characteristics such as skin colour... (b) Discrimination against Africans, and to a lesser extent coloureds and Indians... (c) Segregation of the races in many spheres of life... (d) The legalization and institutionalization of this hierarchical, discriminatory and segregated system, which was enshrined in law and enforced by the government." (Lipton 1986:14–15)

Apartheid evolved from British colonialism in the form of segregatory acts and later received its name by Dr. Hendrik Fransch Verwoerd when he became Prime Minister in 1958. The main thrust of apartheid was to promote economic nationalism among Afrikaners in the form of a secret cultic organisation called *Afrikaner Broederbond* (Afrikaner Brotherhood). The Afrikaners felt that they were a chosen race and instilled an intergenerational sense of being imbued with a sacred history. In this regard, Dr. D. F. Malan said:

> "Our history is the greatest masterpiece of the centuries. We hold this nationhood as our due for it was given us by the Architect of the universe. [His] aim was the formation of a new nation among the nations of the world... The last hundred years have witnessed a miracle behind which must lie a divine plan. Indeed, the history of the Afrikaner reveals a will and a determination which makes one feel that Afrikanerdom is not the work of men but the creation of God." (Cited in Moodie 1980:1)

In light of the above citation it is evident that some Afrikaners felt that they had a divine mission to fulfil in South Africa due to their history, which they regarded to have been guided by the hand of God. What characterised their way of thinking was the idea that they were a special race, set apart by God. This nursed an illusion that they were a special people who should have ultimate control of all economic and political power.

This myth also resulted in disastrous consequences for South African economics and politics. According to this myth the Afrikaner, like the Israel of old that was taken as a vinestock from Egypt and planted and nurtured in Canaan, was taken by God's Providence from Holland, France and Germany and planted and nurtured as a people in Africa. As a result of this, Africans were regarded as heathens who were supposed to be servants to the Afrikaner people. Andre du Toit expands upon this idea:

> "Trekboers on the frontier invoked the curse of Ham on belief that blacks were creatures not fully human to support the view that blacks were destined to be perpetual hewers of wood and drawers of water... Such views are compatible with the notion of the Afrikaner themselves as a Chosen people... The non-whites of South Africa were identified therefore not only with the children

of Ham but with the Canaanites of the Promised Land." (Du Toit 1983:922–928)

This religious teaching became the foundation of apartheid. According to the worldview of apartheid, indigenous Africans were subhumans who were not supposed to engage in any political and economic competition with the Caucasian races. In South Africa, Afrikaners went on to form companies that were mainly aimed at uplifting Afrikaner people to the exclusion of the majority of the indigenous Africans. Under apartheid, the dominant belief was that indigenous African people should never be allowed to set up businesses in areas that were dominated by Caucasian people. Indigenous Africans were excluded from meaningful participation in the mainstream economy. Apartheid was thus a rather systematised racial prejudice against the indigenous South Africans that was economically aimed at providing some rational justification for ethnic greed. Lipton observed the following:

> *"It now seems widely agreed among scholars that the behavior of white South Africans does not, alas, diverge much from the behavior of comparable groups in other societies, faced with competition for resources from people readily distinguished from themselves by colour, culture or religion, and that the key to their behavior must be sought primarily in structural (i.e. social, economic and political) rather than in psychological or ideological factors." (Lipton 1986:11)*

However, it is imperative to note that apartheid was based on the extremist political implementation of ethnic exceptionalism of Afrikaner people as a divinely chosen people to the denigration and total economic deprivation of other ethnic indigenous ethnic communities in South Africa. Inevitably, the economic and political behaviour of most of the white people (who were economic beneficiaries of apartheid) became extremely inhumane since apartheid was adjudged to be an intrinsically evil political system. Apartheid was not about ethnic competition for scarce resources, but the institutionalisation of utmost greed. With unbridled access to the economic opportunities that were provided by the minority racist apartheid government, the majority of white South Africans became psychologically blinded to the economic and political plight of the majority of non-white South Africans.

As demonstrated in the psychology of greed, a person consumed by it can easily ignore the economic needs of the other person. Depriving others of the basic necessities of life can best be described as malevolence. In this regard, Amelie Rorty's characterisation of evil is pertinent. Rorty says, "Evil may not be an ontological category or natural kind, but it seems a fundamental feature of human psychology that (on the whole, normally, other things being equal, etc.) we are revolted by actions that we classify as 'abominable', 'evil', 'inhuman'. Indeed, we are often so horrified by such actions that we aver our eyes and minds from them and yet, in truth, we are also fascinated, even lured by them" (Rorty 2001:xv–xvi). All those who have protested against the expropriation of land and apartheid policies have characterised such practices as intrinsically evil. To put it pragmatically, apartheid was not about racism, ethnicity and nationalism. Rather, it was about the Afrikaner people's expression of greed through rules that entrenched the exclusion of other non-white South African communities from sharing in the wealth of the nation. The same could be said about colonialism or imperialism. Concepts such as racism, ethnicity, and nationalism are usually used to sanitise collectivised greed.

In the case of South Africa, this collectivisation of greed was facilitated by what became known as Afrikaner nationalism, popularly known as the *Broederbond* (brotherhood). The first Economic Congress of the People which was held for the Afrikaners only initiated a process of reflecting on the economic status of the Afrikaners after the Second World War. For example, J. D. Kestell summed the spirit of this *Volkskongres* as follows: "We must look after each other, because we are blood of each other's blood. We belong to each other—we, the small Boer nation, here

29

in South Africa. This drives us to rush to the aid of those of our brothers and sisters who are in need; to help them to help themselves. We do this in the firm belief that we as a people should save ourselves" (Cited in Deklerk 1975:281–282).

With the ascendancy of the Nationalist Party in power, economic nationalism aimed to render economic assistance only to those who were Afrikaners. The rigid enactment of apartheid laws was partly aimed at protecting or hedging the economic interests of the Afrikaner people, and in most cases at the exclusion of black South Africans, who were driven to economically unproductive parts of South Africa called 'home-lands'. As time went by, the socialist Afrikaner economic nationalism metamorphosed into incorporating black Africans from homelands back into the economy, but only as cheap sources of labour.

However, it should not go without saying that the growth of Afri-kaner economic nationalism was partly accentuated by British imperial economic interests in South Africa, which excluded the majority of the Afrikaner population to the fringes of the economy. As De Kiewiet ob-served, "At the base of white society had gathered, like a sediment, a race of men so abject in their poverty, so wanting in resourcefulness, that they stood dangerously close to the native themselves" (Cited in Adam and Giliomee 1983:146). As a reaction to British economic imperialism, Afrikaners formed their own companies such as Santam, Sanlam and Av-bob. Hermann Giliomee bluntly points out: "Some of these enterprises openly appealed to Afrikaner sentiment and solidarity. Sometime later the Afrikaner Teachers Association recommended Sanlam's policies to their members" (Giliomee 1983:147). Colonial capitalism was there-fore partly aimed at the segregation of people based on the determin-ing factors of race and colour. Legislations were put in place with the goal of advancing the economic interests and the voracity of colonialists. Through these self-serving colonial and apartheid policies, the majority of indigenous African people were expropriated not only of land, but of all other economic means for an adequate livelihood. Sol Plaatje observed that a barrage of laws regarding the expropriation of land made it "illegal for natives to live on farms except as servants in the employ of Europeans. He [the native] can only live in town as a servant in the employ of Europeans" (Plaatje 2007:58). The laws of expropriation during the era of colonialism provided a lethal blow to modern capitalism, which the white man supposedly brought to Africa.

Due to the laws of expropriation that dovetailed colonialism, it can be deduced that over the passage of time, colonial capitalism created a dynamic whereby Africans understood themselves as labourers whilst whites were exclusively perceived as employers. Up to the present day, the term 'worker' denotes an indigenous African. The main reason for this is that the advent of capitalism in colonial Africa was accompanied by a work ethic that prized acquisitiveness without hard labour. According to Ali Mazrui, "Capitalism arrived in Africa with the imperative of acquisition without the discipline of work and frugality. The white man himself in Africa set a dangerous example. He never washed his own clothes, or cooked his own food, or polished his own shoes, or made his own bed, or cleaned his own room, or even poured his own gin and tonic" (Mazrui 1990:493). In his earlier work Mazrui said, "The greatest mockery about Western imperialism does not lie in its promotion of capitalism in Africa, it lies in its failure to do so. The West destroyed traditional African economies without really creating capitalist foundations to replace them. In this sense, the problem of dependency in Africa is about who controls capitalism within Africa, rather than about the merits of capitalism" (Mazrui 1986:215). Thus, according to Mazrui, the mediation of capitalism in Africa through colonialism was oriented towards acquisition of material things through expropriation without hard work and frugality.

In the embryonic stages of capitalism in Africa, the idea of not working and simultaneously claiming ownership to that which has been produced by others came to be associated with being in control of the means of production. Within such a context, it can be deduced that the colonial work ethic accorded superiority and laziness to white people. Since the days of colonialism, it was commonly perceived that white people were hoarding all the money whilst indigenous Africans worked for it; thus the phrase '*umlungu wami*' (Zulu) or '*murungu wangu*' (Shona) is sometimes used to refer to someone who has money, be they black or white (Murove 2008:88). The references to a moneyed person in these phrases reflects the normalisation of inequality in society and the internalisation of the reality that only white people were deserving or destined to have money and to be richer than their black counterparts.

Some African scholars and nationalists have argued that colonial capitalism was a spectacular failure in the African context. As Mazrui reflects:

> "In what sense did Western imperialism fail to create African capitalism? The answer lies in the phenomenon of distorted capitalist transmission. Western imperialism transmitted capitalist greed to Africa, but without capitalist discipline. It transmitted the profit motive, but without capitalist discipline. It transmitted the profit motive, but not entrepreneurial persistence and risk-taking." (Mazrui 1986:215)

The transmission of capitalism to Africa was thus merged by the distortion of some of its fundamental principles, such as discipline and entrepreneurial spirit. It is also important to consider the role that was played by African culture in the distortion of the transmission of capitalism in imperialism. For example, African traditional values placed great emphasis on collectivism as opposed to the individualistic dexterity which goes hand in hand with the spirit of entrepreneurship. Equally, the spirit of greed which is indispensable to capitalism was prohibited in African traditional society. In fact, unbridled wealth acquisition without regard for the community and the surrounding family was frowned upon. In this regard it can be said African traditional values have aided imperial capitalism in Africa by putting emphasis on collectivism as opposed to individualism, and that the condemnation of greed in traditional African society has inhibited the appropriation of capitalism. However, colonialism cannot be said to have mediated the spirit of capitalism in Africa; instead, what was bequeathed was a greed-driven spirit of expropriation and exclusion.

Colonial Capitalism and the Culture of Expropriation and Exclusion

Colonial capitalism promoted a culture of expropriation which was logically followed by the exclusion of those whose land and other natural resources had been seized. However, since the worldview of capitalism is instrumentalised, mechanistic and functionalistic, the idea of classifying Africans as clans and tribes became expedient to this capitalistic worldview for reasons which shall be expounded in the following discussion. The colonial economy was organised around the principle of tribalism or ethnicity. In what was then known as Rhodesia, N. H. Wilson read a paper titled *The Development of Native Reserves* to the Rhodesian Scientific Association in January 1923. As a way of stressing the importance of introducing Native Reserves, Wilson said the following:

> "We may educate the native with education—literary, industrial, religious, liberal and vocational; we may uplift him until individual natives are on a plane with Booker Washington; but unless we have some field of activity to which he may pass on we shall not only break the machine, but we ourselves shall be buried under the debris." (Wilson 1923:86)

The creation of Native Reserves was primarily based on economic considerations that were aimed at depriving Africans of any access to the material resources of the country. As shown previously, Native Reserves were areas that were not suitable for human habitation. The creation of Native Reserves or homelands, as in the case of apartheid South Africa, was aimed at ensuring that indigenous Africans would enjoy as little economic benefit as possible. For example, in the cases of Rhodesia and apartheid South Africa, white people captured all the fertile lands and commercially strategic areas, bringing total deprivation to the Africans.

In this process, the concept of the tribe or ethnic group was applied as an organising principle for economic deprivation of indigenous African people. For example, Wilson gave two objectives for the creation of Native Reserves in Rhodesia: "Firstly, the full economic development of the native as a unit of the State; secondly, the development of the native in such a way that they will come as little as possible in conflict or competition with the white man socially, economically and politically" (Wilson 1923:87). Under apartheid, Africans were classified as tribes who resided in colonially statutory specified tribal areas that were largely aimed at excluding them from meaningful participation in the economy. Whilst capitalism is based on the idea of a free and competitive market, one finds that colonial or apartheid legislations were enacted in a way that deliberately prohibited economic competition between the European settler community and the indigenous Africans. Africans were divided into reserves where they were then organised into tribes, which subsequently made it possible for the colonisers to turn African people into labour units and to actively promote their own economic interests (Murove 1999:45–46). In light of the above observation, the idea of categorising Africans in terms of tribes and ethnic groupings is thus a colonial invention that helped to advance the economic interests of the colonisers.

Apart from the fact that the arbitrary colonial borders drawn during the Berlin Conference in 1884 led to a separation of erstwhile similar ethnic groups, there was also an economic logic to the instrumentalisation of ethnicity by colonisers. Thus, Africans were categorised with the tacit aim of sanctioning against racial integration equal and economic opportunities within a capitalistic free market economic system. It is partly on these grounds that one finds that tribes were defined as cultural units possessing a common language, a single social system, and an established common law. The notion of common law had disastrous economic implications for the majority of the African populace. On the basis of common law, Africans were deprived of private ownership of land. The world-renowned historian, Terrence Ranger, observed that:

> "The reinforcement of ethnicity and greater rigidity of social definition were the necessary and unplanned consequences of colonial economic and political change—of the breakup of internal patterns of trade and communication, the defining of territorial boundaries and the alienation of land, the establishment of Reserves. But some part of them were the result of conscious determination on the part of the colonial authorities to re-establish order and security and a sense of community by means of defining and enforcing tradition." (Ranger 1993:243)

The colonial organisation of Africans into tribes or ethnic groupings was a process that was deliberately imposed on the Africans by the colonialists. From a Marxist perspective, Archie Mafeje argued that the colonial reorganisation of African societies had some economic and political underpinnings and that during the time of colonialism, "African societies were being drawn into a complex of extractive economic and political relations, the effects of which could not be ignored even by most tribal-fixated anthropologists" (Mafeje 1971:254). For economic reasons, African people who belonged to different communities were usually driven into areas where they found themselves lumped together under the authority of a chosen chief. Mafeje went on to say that in modern times, tribalism—which is a false consciousness—is used for economic purposes. He writes, "On the part of the new African elite, it is a ploy or distortion they use to conceal their exploitative role" (Mafeje 1971:259). The ideology of tribalism has oftentimes served the economic interests of a few of the African elite who appeal to this ideology when they want to hoard wealth for themselves. For example, some politicians in post-colonial Africa have staffed government departments with tribesmen with the aim of facilitating swift looting of government resources.

In the post-colonial African context, the legacy of tribalism has given rise to the idea that natural resources that are found in a particular area of the country should be owned and controlled by the tribe or the ethnic group residing in that area. For example, in post-apartheid South Africa, there is a Platinum Belt that stretches from Pretoria up to the North-Western Province. When one travels in this area there are signs stating that the Platinum Belt belongs to the Royal Bafokeng tribe; hence, mining companies are expected to pay royalties to this tribe. However, it does not hold true that the whole area containing platinum is only populated by the Bafokeng tribe.

The idea of attributing national resources to tribal ownership tends to compromise the reality of national ownership of natural resources. During the times of colonialism, the same idea was used in a way that was intended to create the impression that homelands or Native Reserves were economically self-sustaining. Such a system helped to ward off pressure on the colonial mainstream economy. On the other hand, the concept of a tribe helped to destroy the spirit of private land ownership because the whole land was deemed to belong to the tribe as a whole. Therefore, the term 'Tribal Trust land' implied that the tribe owned the land and not the individual who was making use of it. Economically, tribalism disempowered African people from ownership of land. This implies that Africans could not access loans from banks because they lacked surety. Tribal land could not be considered as capital because it lacked individual ownership.

Due to the legacy of colonialism, the issue of tribalism has partly contributed to economic decay in post-colonial Africa. Sometimes economic opportunities are given to individuals on the basis of their tribal affiliation instead of their inherent economic capabilities. From an ethnic perspective, traits such as language, religion, custom, etiquette and dress and a shared primordial origin are considered to be of paramount importance (Sithole 1985:184). Masipula Sithole argued against Clifford Geertz, who hypothesised that tribalism in Africa was primordial or that it dominated motivations in politics. Sithole debunked this hypothesis by advancing the argument that:

> "[People] are socialized into ethnicity as they are into religious prejudice, racism, sexism, and the like. Moreover, ethnicity, like many other social phenomena, is intermittent. Its salience changes, depending on situations, issues involved, and on interpretations given to issues by particular actors. The drive or motivation to invoke 'tribal ideology', or to organize on ethnic lines, is not always active. It usually remains dormant or latent and is activated by particular circumstances." (Sithole 1985:185)

According to Sithole, there are factors that trigger tribal tendencies in Africans. Among some of the factors identified are economics and politics. Economically, "if the rate of economic growth declines, ethnic identity will become more salient. This is due to competition over scarce resources, or in this case, a shrinking pie. Thus, in a booming economy, one expects the salience of ethnicity to be held in check by lowered competition through the greater availability of resources" (Ibid, 185).

However, Sithole's argument is unsustainable as it downplays the role that was played by colonialism and anthropologists in the creation of ethnic or tribal identities in Africa. Here I am more concerned with how tribalism has been practised in the post-colonial African economy in a way that has consequently destroyed it. Many leaders in the African continent are known for surrounding themselves with so-called tribesmen under the mistaken impression that their loyalty will automatically translate into economic success. On the other hand, surrounding oneself with tribesmen gives political leaders easy access to looting national wealth. Thus, tribalism impedes economic progress because the whole economy is usually subjected to a network of nepotism and patronage, which sacrifices objectivity when giving an authentic analysis of the actual state of the economy.

Another type of conduct that was mediated to the African continent via colonialism is related to greed and usually manifests itself in the form of corruption. In contemporary Africa, greed has often appeared in this form. In such instances, a public figure or politician sees his purpose of being in office as that of enriching himself through hoarding of ill-gotten wealth. Ascendancy into public office is seen as a golden opportunity to loot as much as possible from public coffers in a way that has no limits. It sometimes manifests itself in a way that can be likened to a pack of hyenas ravenously feeding on the carcass of a donkey.

In the case of South Africa, this type of economic behaviour can be traced back to colonialism and apartheid. Thus, white people gave themselves privileged positions that legalised the looting of national resources without restraint. The ethical ideal of juxtaposing public office with public accountability remained a fantasy during the colonial era. The economic cake was exclusively and jealously guarded for the good of the runaway appetites of the white settler community. Thus, one finds that greed was institutionalised in the colonial or apartheid political system. Fertile areas of land with mineral-rich soil—the most lucrative form of business—became the natural and exclusive preserve of the white settler community. Under colonialism and apartheid in Southern Africa, no white person was ever accused or investigated for the embezzlement of public coffers. Such actions were unnecessary since corruption constituted the heart of the colonial legal framework.

The question that arises out of this is whether colonial or imperial capitalism has culminated with Africa's attainment of independence. In short, it would be naïve for one to think so. While colonialists or imperialists might have ceded political power, they have maintained a steady grip on economic power within their prior colonies where they promote their economic self-interest and self-indulgence. In 1965, Kwame Nkrumah wrote a book entitled *Neo-Colonialism: The Last Stage of Imperialism*, which remains just as relevant today. In this book, Nkrumah emphasises the resilience of neo-colonialism:

> "The neo-colonialism of today represents imperialism in its final
> and perhaps most dangerous stage. In the past, it was possible to

convert a country upon which a neo-colonial regime had been imposed. Today this process is no longer feasible. Old-fashioned colonialism is by no means entirely abolished. It still constitutes an African problem, but it is everywhere on the retreat. Once a territory has become nominally independent it is no longer possible, as it was in the last century, to reverse the process. In place of colonialism as the main instrument of imperialism we have today neo-colonialism. The essence of neo-colonialism is that the State which is subject to it is, in theory, independent and has all the outward trappings of international sovereignty. In reality, its economic system and thus its political policy is directed from outside. More often, however, neo-colonialist control is exercised through economic or monetary means." (Nkrumah 1971:ix)

Neo-colonialism through economic control of the previous colonies perpetuates the continuous existence of imperial capitalism or booty capitalism. Countries that are victims of neo-colonialism find themselves trapped in a vicious circle of economic dependence because the imperial power's economic survival depends on extracting resources from the previous colonies. It is for this reason that neo-colonialism thrives on entrenching parasitic relationships with the previous colonies. Under neo-colonialism, previous colonies find themselves in economic relations that make them wholly dependent on former colonial powers through mechanisms such as foreign aid and the financial machinations of external multilateral financial organisations, like the International Monetary Fund (IMF) and the World Bank. These multilateral institutions are known for serving the tradition of booty capitalism for the USA and its Western allies. Nkrumah observed that the former French colonies in Africa are subjected to selective provision of French aid, usually given in a way that is always advantageous for France. He declares, "French African aid originally arose from the advantage which French firms and individuals derived from the African franc zone and this has determined the framework in which the aid is still provided. So long as the relationship which the aid provided was profitable to France it naturally continued" (Nkrumah 1971:17). The idea of providing economic aid is an indirect way of entrenching the imperial practice of booty capitalism. While France may have vacated the political scene as a colonial power, she has held steadfastly to the practice of imperial or colonial booty capitalism through the provision of foreign aid.

Many critics of foreign aid have maintained that it never aimed to alleviate poverty in the recipient countries, but to perpetuate the economic practice of booty capitalism. Foreign aid is a modern way of exercising imperial dominance on the recipient countries. The book by John Perkins, *Confessions of an Economic Hit Man*, ventures into a pragmatic narration of how foreign aid is used to cushion the American world's imperial dominance and predatory economic practices all over the world. On his reflection on foreign aid and its economic impact on less-developed countries in the face of rampant social destitution and economic decay in previously colonised countries, Perkins said:

> "... I pondered the nature of foreign aid, and I considered the legitimate role that developed countries (DC, in the world bank jargon) might play in helping alleviate poverty and misery in less-developed countries (LDCs). I began to wonder when foreign aid is genuine and when it is only greedy and self-serving. Indeed, I began to question whether such aid is ever altruistic, and if not, whether that could be changed." (Perkins 2005:48)

According to Perkins, foreign aid was a mechanism of serving the economic greed of the developed countries and was wholly devoid of any altruistic motives. Thus, in his journal he made the following painful reflection:

> "Is anyone in the U.S. innocent? Although those at the very pinnacle of the economic pyramid gain the most, millions of us depend—either directly or indirectly—on the exploitation of the LDCs [Less Developed Countries] for our livelihoods. The resources and cheap labour that feed nearly all our businesses

come from places like Indonesia, and very little ever makes its
way back. The loans of foreign aid ensure that today's children
and their grandchildren will be held hostage. They will have to
allow our corporations to ravage their natural resources and
will have to forego education, health, and other social services
merely to pay us back. The fact that our own companies already
received most of this money to build the power plants, airports,
and industrial parks does not factor into this formula." (Perkins
2005:48–49)

In light of the above reflection, one can easily deduce that foreign aid benefits those who grant it instead of the recipients. Through the practice of providing foreign aid, the bygone imperial capitalistic practice of expropriation of resources is practised in a rather sophisticated way that enables the developed countries to escape moral censure. Dambisa Moyo is one among several critics of foreign aid, and believes that it has done more harm than good in Africa. Since the 1960s, foreign economic and development advisers descended on Africa and were excessively preoccupied with a Marshall Plan menu for Africa which included an emphasis on capital, technology and capacity transfers, accompanied with a generous supply of economic development advisers.

Since then, several development prescription packages have been developed in the Global North for implementation in Africa. These include Poverty Reduction Strategies (PRSs), Community Development Programmes (CDPs) as well as Rural Reconstruction and Development Programmes (RRDPs), among other initiatives. While development aid can build people's assets, support good governance, and enhance skills and capacities to bring about transformation, the negative aspect of unbridled aid is its potential to contribute to dependency and further underdevelopment of Africa.

In a damning critique of foreign aid, David Karanja, a former Kenyan member of parliament, said:

> *"Foreign aid has done more harm to Africa than we care to admit. It has led to a situation where Africa has failed to set its own pace and direction of development free of external interference. Today, Africa's development plans are drawn thousands of miles away in the corridors of the IMF and World Bank. What is sad is that the IMF and World Bank experts who draw these development plans are people completely out of touch with the local African reality." (Ayittey 1998:275)*

Given the above analysis, one can justifiably say that foreign aid given to poor countries by developed countries is merely a modern form of the booty capitalism that was prevalent during the peak of colonialism. This is pragmatically and bluntly affirmed by Perkins when he says, "We in the DCs were the users of resources; those in the LDCs were the suppliers. It was the colonial mercantile system all over again, set up to make it easy for those with power and limited natural resources to exploit those with resources but no power" (Perkins 2005:49). While less developed countries or previously colonised countries are endowed with an abundance of natural resources, those natural resources are usually taken away by the developed countries in a way that leaves the less developed countries economically destitute. The economic culture of giving foreign aid to previously colonised countries is a political mechanism that has peacefully done away with the idea of independence and sovereignty within the previous colonies. The economic and socio-political viability or functioning of the previously colonised countries is wholly determined by the foreign aid which is given by the developed countries or previous imperial powers. One finds that social goods such as health, education and food security in less developed countries depend on their willingness to provide developed countries with unbridled access to the plundering of their natural resources.

Imperial Capitalism and the Modern Wars

For decades since Africa's independence, there have been several cases where the quest by state and non-state actors to control the continent's natural resources has contributed to resource wars. Indeed, a careful analysis of the factors contributing to the protracted nature of such wars reveals that economic and financial agendas are the underlying reasons for the perpetuation of conflicts in Africa. Modern wars are being fought on the basis of the greed and insatiability of multinational corporations who have captured states all over the world. In Africa, it is evident that private and state actors congregate where there are natural resources that have high value within the international global market. Nowhere is this situation more apparent than the current conflict in the Eastern Congo. The war in the eastern part of the Democratic Republic of Congo is largely driven by the desire of multinational corporations and their capital to access and control the country's vast mineral resources, as well as others. The eastern DRC is rich in mineral resources, including the precious mineral known as coltan (Columbite-Tantalite). Coltan is a rare metallic ore, the ingredients of which are critical for the production of microchips in information and communication technologies such as cellphones and computers. Alongside this, there are several other minerals which have served to ensure that the conflict in DRC endures, including gold, tin and diamonds amongst others.

The DRC case is not unique; it reflects a pattern of how complex conflict can become due to the ulterior motive of greed by multinational corporations and states, who are often the actors in the conflict. The previous political understanding of nation-states as sovereign entities within their territories has been superseded by the idea that it is in actual fact the multinational corporation companies and their economic interests that are the ultimate sovereigns.

The need to secure cheap oil has resulted in the USA and her Western allies sponsoring wars in the Arab world. The war which the USA and her Western allies fought against Saddam Hussein's invasion of Kuwait was mainly driven by their greed to secure easy access to cheap oil. The war was not necessarily about punishing Saddam Hussein's violation of international law when he invaded Kuwait, nor was it about protecting the freedom and human rights of the Kuwait people; it was chiefly concerned with forcibly expelling Hussein and preventing him from monopolising oil in the Gulf region. Kenneth Vaux noted, "When Iraq invaded Kuwait, 20 percent of the world's known oil reserves were in Iraqi hands and by annexing Kuwait and Saudi Arabia, Iraq would increase that to 40 percent. The prospect was intolerable to the West" (Vaux 1992:9). The USA and her Western allies are known to be the main global consumers of energy or oil and most of their companies rely heavily on its cheap availability. Without this cheap oil, most of their gigantic industries would come to a standstill, thus plunging their national economies into a recession and ultimately leading to the decay of their luxurious lifestyles (which the USA and her Western allies usually refer to as their 'way of life').

The demand for cheap oil and its link to contemporary US imperialism is well-observed by David Harvey in his book, *The New Imperialism*. He states, "A narrow conspiracy thesis rests on the idea that the government in Washington is nothing more than an oil mafia that has usurped the public domain. This idea is supported by the close connections of Bush and Cheney to oil interests..." (Harvey 2005:18). In other words, what has prompted the USA to undertake military intervention in the Arab world is the greed for oil.

Saddam Hussein's invasion of Kuwait and the subsequent response of the USA and her allies demonstrated the resilience of imperialism in international relations and how it is primarily geared at perpetuating booty capitalism in our globalised world. The mistake that Hussein made in his invasion of Kuwait was to underestimate this. When the United Nations Security Council authorised the expulsion of Iraqi forces from Kuwait the president of the United States of America, George W. Bush, saw this authorisation as an opportunity to reaffirm the USA's imperial aspirations of pursuing its national interests in the Gulf region.

The war over Kuwait, according to scholars, was launched with ulterior motives such as the removal of Saddam Hussein from political power as well as the plundering of Iraq's oil (See Cockayne and Malone 2010:387; Malone 2006:84–85). The UN and the UN Security Council facilitated the USA and its allies' plundering of Iraq oil when they agreed to the idea that Iraq should be subjected to comprehensive economic sanctions despite having withdrawn from Kuwait.

The Oil-for-Food Programme (OIP), which was put in place by the United Nations Security Council as a mechanism for the alleviation of the humanitarian catastrophe in post-Gulf war Iraq, is a classic example of the USA and her allies' quest for cheap oil being achieved at the expense of genuine humanitarian and moral considerations. This programme was adopted by the United Nations Security Council's Resolution 706. According to this draconian resolution, Iraq was expected to export oil to raise revenue for buying foodstuffs, medicines and other civilian critical needs. When Iraq refused to comply with such a resolution "the US and the UK sponsored a Security Council Resolution 778 which authorized states to seize revenues from Iraq petroleum sales and transfer them to the escrow account provided for in Security Council 706" (Malone 2006:116). This was an unprecedented expropriation of Iraq's oil fronted as humanitarian aid by the United Nations Security Council, whilst subjecting Iraqis, especially children, to a situation of unprecedented suffering. Iraqi people were not helped in the process; instead, the whole aim was to loot Iraq's oil under the pretext of providing humanitarian aid.

Alongside Iraq, Libya has also emerged as a victim of the same imperial aspirations of the USA and her allies. When Colonel Muammar Gaddafi assumed political office after a coup against King Idris, he embarked on the nationalisation of the British Imperial Petroleum Oil Company, which was by then monopolising the plunder of Libyan oil. His nationalisation of Libyan oil for the benefit of the Libyan people turned him into an enemy and he quickly became a target for elimination by the USA and her imperial allies (Pakenham 1991:673). The overthrow of Gaddafi from political office and his subsequent execution was followed by the announcement that post-Gaddafi Libya was brimming with business opportunities for Western imperial companies.

In the aftermath of the overthrow of Gaddafi, Seumas Milne observed that these imperial powers expressed uncontrollable excitement at the prospect of having access to Libyan oil wells. He writes, "No wonder the new British defense secretary is telling businessmen to 'pack their bags' for Libya, and the US ambassador in Tripoli insists American companies are needed on a 'big scale'" (Milne 2012:240). The main objective in the overthrow of Gaddafi from power was not necessarily about enabling a political environment that would allow the flourishing of democracy; rather, it created a situation whereby the USA and her Western allies could freely plunder Libyan oil. The whole UNSC Resolution (1973), which stressed the importance of enforcing a 'no-fly zone' for the protection of civilians, was in actual fact about overthrowing Gaddafi from power to eliminate any hindrance to Western powers when exploiting the rich Libyan oil wells. The idea of a no-fly zone was claimed to protect civilians but in reality, it assisted the overthrow of Gaddafi, by ensuring that the Libyan government would not be able to enforce law and order in its own territory. Constantino Chiwenga aptly observed, "The enforcement of a no-fly zone carried with it the arming of Western sponsored rebels who were fighting on the ground against Libyan forces. In the unfolding of events, NATO's aim was to overthrow President Gaddafi's government, not to protect civilians" (Chiwenga 2014:125).

The USA's global imperial dominance must ultimately be achieved through absolute control of oil wealth in the Arab world. Thus far, most of the oil-rich Arab countries have been turned into buffer states and the only countries that remain a stumbling block are Syria and Iran. The current ongoing destruction of Syria through USA and NATO-sponsored mercenaries is aimed at the destruction of Iran, because it is the strongest remaining military power among the Arab countries in the Middle East. Once Iran has been destroyed, the USA's control of Arab oil will be complete. This is important as the country that controls the world's energy resources will be considered the real imperial power. In sum, the Middle East conflict is not about fighting terrorism nor is it about bringing democracy to the Arab world. It is fundamentally rooted in the desire of Western imperial powers to control the source of the world's energy through plunder. This is the main source of modern imperialism and the main reason for wars being fought in the Arab world.

The globalisation of neoliberal capitalism allowed developed countries to prey on poor or underdeveloped countries. This is the observation that was made by James Petras and Henry Veltmeyer with reference to the USA's imperial relationship with Latin America. According to these authors:

> "The imperially designed neoliberal model led to a long-term and large-scale systematic pillage of every country in Latin America with resources to pillage. Calculations from data provided by the Economic Commission for Latin America and the Caribbean (ECLAC) (2002a and 2000b) on remittances for payments of profit and interest, show that returns on the operations of US capital in Latin America averaged close to $60 billion a year in the 1990s. Over the decade, $585 billion in interest payments and profits were remitted to the centre of the empire, the vast bulk of it to US home offices." (Petras and Veltmeyer 2005:55)

In this economic relationship, the USA is able to carry out the ferocious looting of Latin American resources.

One also finds that through the recommended neoliberal capitalistic economic policies of IMF and World Bank, most underdeveloped countries have made themselves indebted in a way that ensures they remain under the claws of the imperial powers and depend on the assistance of these multilateral financial institutions. IMF and World Bank loans have

47

created a socio-economic political situation of perennial rule over most underdeveloped countries, and as a result, these countries have been unable to disentangle themselves from the suffocating claws of imperialism. It is imperative to note that the so-called underdeveloped countries are usually endowed with an abundance of natural resources and yet they remain poor or economically destitute. In contemporary times, imperial powers have refused to agree that their own economic policies—that are tailored to promote their imperial greed at the expense of the poor— are the cause of poverty and civil wars in poor countries. Rather, they suggest that the cause of poverty is due to the absence of foreign aid, investment and jobs.

Deepening Imperial Claws through Foreign Aid, Investment and Jobs

Developed countries have deepened their imperial claws in poor countries by spreading the notion that they are benevolent due to the foreign aid they sometimes extend to them. Poor countries are required to enact foreign direct investment policies with the hope that this foreign investment will later create jobs for their citizens. At face value, foreign aid gives the impression that the giver of aid is only doing so out of generosity. However, on further analysis, many scholars have come to the conclusion that this foreign aid is usually intended to ensnare the recipient in order to fulfil the long-term economic aims of the aid giver. The imperial economic aim behind foreign aid is aptly expressed in the adage that says 'Rather than give a man a fish, one should teach him how to fish'. However, the lesson on how to fish comes in the form of helping the recipient to devise economic and political policies that attract Foreign Direct Investment. In order to attract this, the poorer countries are usually advised to enact policies that are, to put mildly, 'investor friendly'. However, a pragmatic analysis into the real meaning of 'investor friendliness' reveals that poor countries are indirectly coerced into doing away with all the laws that are intended to protect them.

The idea of sacrificing the poor has been a salient feature in IMF and World Bank lending policies. One finds that at the macro-economic level, these financial institutions have always insisted that African, Latin American and Asiatic governments should cut spending on welfare and not interfere with the market. On the macro-economic level, these governments are encouraged to promulgate policies that allow for the mobility of capital (Murove 2008:136–137). While the mantra of foreign direct investment is conducive to job creation, the experience of poor countries is that it has degenerated into a euphemism for exploitation of the poor as the foreign investor is primarily there to reap maximum profits at the expense of the host country. Investors do not necessarily invest their capital in underdeveloped countries with the aim of creating jobs, but to loot resources from those underdeveloped countries.

Imperial capitalism in underdeveloped countries is thus perpetuated through the practice of foreign aid and foreign direct investment. These are mechanisms that enable imperial powers to stealthily loot the resources of underdeveloped countries. Graham Hancock's book, *Lords of Poverty*, lucidly elaborates on how foreign aid is used by modern imperial powers to plunder the resources of poor countries in a way that defies any altruistic sentiment, despite the claim of its proponents that the practice is an expression of moral concern for the sufferings of others. Hancock critiqued foreign aid as follows:

> *"While it would be convenient to believe that the decision to launch large-scale aid programs was the product of clear uniform thinking on the part of the industrialized nations in the post-war era, the truth is otherwise. From the outset, a number of quite different motivations were at work—and at work side by side. The result, today, is that the collective psychology of aid-giving is schizophrenic, shot through with contradictory urges and rationalizations, some of which are benign, some sinister and others just plain neurotic." (Hancock 1989:69)*

While the advocates of foreign aid justify this practice as being aimed at alleviating human suffering and promoting economic development in poor countries, the motives behind the practice of foreign aid is imbued with imperial motives of plundering the resources of its recipients. Hancock went on to observe that advocates of foreign aid advertise the importance of foreign aid as not only "morally right to do so, but also could be good for business" (Hancock 1989:70). Foreign aid is not concerned with morality; rather, it is focused on promoting economic and political imperial aspirations of the giver to the recipient.

According to Hancock, the United Nations gatherings have become the legitimising arena whereby powerful empires pursue their imperial dreams. He avers:

> *"Whatever noble mission the United Nations may once have had has, I am now convinced, long since been forgotten in the rapid proliferation of its self-perpetuating bureaucracies—in the seemingly endless process by which empires have been created within the system by ambitious and greedy men and then staffed by time-servers and sycophants. Rather than encouraging humility and dedication, the world body's structure seems to be actively rewarding self-seeking behavior and providing staff with many opportunities to abuse the grave responsibilities with which they have been entrusted." (Hancock 1989:84)*

The United Nations has thus become a multilateral institution which is nursing imperial dreams and greed instead of serving the common good of humanity. The organs of the United Nations have been wholly compromised due to the culture of economic aid. Modern imperial powers such as the USA use their aid to pursue their parochial national interest, in stark contrast to the common good of the UN as a multilateral organisation founded on the ideal of ensuring peaceful co-existence among humanity. Due to greed, this multilateral organisation has been reduced to an arena where insatiable appetites for material wealth and political power have resulted in perennial strife, all in quest of ultimate domination of the whole world. Those who are members of the United Nations are enticed by pecuniary material benefits that ensure they act in a way that is in sync with the imperial aspirations of the USA. This is an unavoidable trap for members of the United Nations, since the US dollar is the universal currency!

Here again Hancock cannot be surpassed in his description when he characterises the travelling opportunities for the United Nations personnel as analogous to travelling on a gravy train.

> "Official [UN] travel is thus a gravy train (or perhaps a jumbo jet) on which everyone wants to book a seat. Far from efforts being made to cut down on costs in this area the UN seems dedicated to search out every possible opportunity to spend more. All in all, the habit of sending its staff on ever more frequent overseas trips now costs the United Nations system almost $100 million a year, which is more than the value of the annual exports of several developing countries." (Hancock 1989:91)

Thus, those who profess to have dedicated their energies to helping the poor in the UN system are not necessarily helping them, but are actually enriching themselves. This is very significant as it demonstrates that the rationale of greed is partly based on depriving those who are less fortunate from having a decent livelihood.

Greed and Imperialism

An argument that is usually advanced by imperial powers is that the countries that they colonise are not morally responsible. This clamour to moral responsibility provides a justification for plundering the resources of the colonised or declaring a war against them in the face of resistance amidst scarce world resources. It is a practice one finds prevalent in British imperialism, whereby the colonised were often described as endowed with an infantile intellect whilst the imperialists portrayed themselves as representatives of human adulthood par excellence. This paternalistic outlook implicitly suggested that the colonised did not know how to use their natural resources for their own advancement and thus required guidance from the colonisers, who were required to bequeath modern capitalistic practices to the colonised. This made it both natural and moral for the imperial power to make decisions on behalf of the colonised. During the height of British imperialism the chairman of Lever Brothers at the time, Lord Leverhulme, expressed this mode of paternalistic imperial moral responsibility at a dinner that was held at Liverpool Chamber of Commerce in 1924:

> "I am certain that the West African races have to be treated very much as one would treat children when they are immature and underdeveloped. We have excellent materials. I don't know better materials anywhere for labour in the tropics than the natives of West Africa but they are not organized. Now the organizing ability is the particular trait and characteristic of the white man. I say this with my little experience that the African native will be happier, produce the best, and live under the larger conditions of prosperity when his labour is directed and organized by his white brother who has all these million years' start ahead of him." (Cited in Davis 1973:385)

In such utterances, it is undeniably clear that imperialists camouflaged greed under the guise of moral responsibility.

John Hobson, whose work has been regarded by critics of imperialism such as Vladimir Lenin and Kwame Nkrumah, refuted the argument of justifying imperialism on moral grounds when he observed that British imperialism was connected to the business interests of a small clique of business people. He regarded this small business clique as "economic parasites of imperialism" that benefitted from Britain's imperial adventures. Hobson observed, "Certain definite business and professional interests feeding upon imperialistic expenditure, or upon the results of that expenditure, are thus set up in opposition to the common good, and, instinctively feeling their way to one another, are found united in strong sympathy to support every new imperialist exploit" (Hobson 1948:48). Modern imperialism was not a national democratic undertaking by the British citizens, but rather a result of "the combination of economic and political forces". Hobson states unequivocally that: "The forces are traced to their sources in the selfish interests of certain industrial, financial, and professional classes, seeking private advantages out of a policy of imperial expansion, and using this same policy to protect them in their economic, political, and social privileges against the pressure of democracy" (Hobson 1948:196). The urge to undertake imperial adventures was not necessarily something that was supported by the whole of the British population but by groups of business people who found the exercise profitable.

However, this does not suggest that Britain was not profiteering from imperialism. As Hobson put it, "By far the most important economic factor in Imperialism is the influence relating to investments. The growing cosmopolitanism of capital has been the greatest economic change of recent generations. Every advanced industrial nation has been tending to place a larger share of its capital outside the limits of its own political area, in foreign countries, or in colonies, and to draw a growing income from this source" (Hobson 1948:51). Thus, imperialism constituted the main source of the imperial power's foreign investment as it was from those colonies that the imperial power extracted wealth in the form of raw materials. These raw materials were later sold to the colonies as finished products at exorbitant rates.

Imperial powers have often accused each other of being treacherous and hypocritical for presenting imperialism as an important vehicle for the spread of Christianity and civilization. It is on the basis of Christianity and civilization that the argument of the moral zeal or responsibility of imperialists mostly hinges. Africans were commonly characterised in colonial historiographies as savages who were entangled in heinous, sinful practices. According to Hobson, imperialism was not purely driven by the dark economic motive of greed. Thus, he observed:

> *"There exists in a considerable though not a large proportion of the British nation a genuine desire to spread Christianity among the heathen, to diminish the cruelty and other sufferings which they believe exist in countries less fortunate than their own, and to do good work about the world in the cause of humanity. Most of the churches contain a small body of men and women deeply, even passionately, interested in such work, and a much larger number whose sympathy, though weaker, is quite genuine."*
> *(Hobson 1948:197)*

While missionaries and other philanthropists believed that Christianity and the goods of Western civilization were good for those people whom they perceived to be backward, Hobson noted that "the selfish forces" which direct "imperialism" utilised "the protective colours" of these imperially disinterested movements (Ibid). Thus, imperialist politicians, soldiers and company directors "simply and instinctively attach to themselves any strong, genuine elevated feeling which is of service, fan it and feed it until it assumes fervour, and utilize it for their ends" (Ibid). Missionaries and philanthropists were used by hardcore imperialists such as politicians and businessmen to pursue their own selfish interests. The folly of imperialism lay in the fact that those who undertook it justified their actions on the basis that it was a morally benevolent gesture committed towards humanity in the form of spreading Christianity and civilization.

Historian and avid defender of colonialism, Alfred J. Hanna, finds some moral justification for imperialism and colonialism: "Africans would still be roughly what they were a century ago, had it not been for the introduction of European administration, European instruction, and contact with the European economy." Hanna went on to lambaste those who critiqued the element of greed in imperialism when he said that such a critique was simply based on "elementary misconception" because "[t]he mineral and other resources of Africa were useless to the native inhabitants until they were developed [by imperialists] and they could not be developed without transport, machinery and skill. By making these things available the European investor, however self-interested he may have been, was serving Africa" (Hanna 1961:11–71). It can be deduced that Hanna argued that imperialism was actually benevolent to Africa because upon final analysis, it was the African who benefited economically, even though benevolence might not have been the primary motive for the imperialists. This way of thinking, as we shall see in the following chapter, is also entrenched within modern capitalism. The following chapter sheds light on how modern capitalism teaches that we should not be concerned with the motives behind the actions that are taken by people; rather we should consider the outcome. Christianity and civilization were the products of imperialism. But was imperialism genuinely concerned with Christianity and civilization?

Hobson noticed that there was a psychological problem related to the conceptualisation of imperialism regarding whether it was morally justifiable or not.

> "The psychical problem which confronts us in the advocates of the mission of Imperialism is certainly no case of hypocrisy, or of deliberate conscious simulation of false motives. It is partly the dupery of imperfectly realized ideas, partly a case of psychical departmentalism. Imperialism has been floated on a sea of vague, shifty, well-sounding phrases which are seldom tested by close contact with fact." (Hobson 1948:206)

Thus, according to Hobson, there was no common moral ground for the justification of imperialism because of the prior existence of a combination of motives. When Cecil John Rhodes set up a company that was poised on conquering the interior of Southern Africa, he did so under the guise of the need to expand the British Empire. However, on the unfolding of events when he entered the interior of the Limpopo, he was only interested in finding another gold reef that would create a tremendous opportunity for the expansion of his personal wealth. The subsequent naming of that area of South Africa 'Rhodesia' after himself reflects the idea that the British Empire was used as a cover for individualistic and self-serving purposes. Thus, imperialism offered ample opportunity to pursue individual greed.

There is no doubt that in the modern world, the USA is playing the imperial role that was once undertaken by Britain. With the collapse of the Soviet Union and communism, the USA has risen to unprecedented preternatural domination. Previously, British imperialism left room for its colonies to determine their own political and economic policies. Currently, however, the imperial hegemony of the USA is imposed on countries that are deemed to be against USA policies in the form of economic sanctions and sometimes through military force. In most cases, this is done in the relentless pursuit of what it deems to be national self-interest.

Countries are usually befriended by the USA on the basis of their foreign policy contribution to the USA's national interest, or what its politicians deem to be its national greed. The electoral campaign slogan of current American president, Donald Trump, was 'America First', unashamedly demonstrating that American national interest would be prioritised in all his international relations. Trump was reminding the world that his main purpose in office as an imperial power of the world was to serve American greed at any cost. But what President Trump trumpets as his own foreign policy is not necessarily his own personal invention. President Lyndon Baines Johnson is on record for saying that, "America's only interests in the world today are those we regard as inseparable from our moral duties to mankind" (See Darby 1987:169). The inherent problem in such a dictum is that it conflates morality with American national interest, according to which all of humanity is supposed to be judged. As a result, the USA's imperial tentacles are currently being felt in all the multilateral organisations such as the UN, UNSC, the World Bank and the International Monetary Fund. Theodore von Laue poignantly observed the USA's world imperial dominance as follows:

> "During its first decade and a half the United Nations was pa-
> tently an instrument of American policy counterbalancing its
> Cold War hard line. With the help of the United Nations the
> United States could magnify its peaceful post-war outreach and
> achieve a universal presence, preparing the way for reshaping
> the world after its own image. The United States at the outset
> paid 40% of the UN budget; it supported the largest delegation. It
> succeeded in establishing the UN headquarters in the New York
> City, the metropolitan centre of the world and the most desirable
> assignment, especially for Third World diplomats. From the UN
> headquarters, American goods and styles of living radiated into
> the world, establishing the United States as a worldwide model of
> the good life..." [my emphasis] (Von Laue 1987:320)

The USA's imperial aspirations have been tied to the desire for all countries to emulate its own national economic and political values, such
as the free market and multiparty democracy. As shown previously, the
countries that emulate these values are usually rewarded with US aid.

It is beyond any doubt that the USA has advanced its imperial policies through its world economic dominance. This world economic dominance is expressed in the promulgation of economic policies that are
usually aimed at forcing poor countries to adopt the desired USA neoliberal capitalistic policies. The former president of the USA, Bill Clinton,
is on record for promoting the economic policy called African Growth
Opportunity Act (AGOA), a policy which is purported to promote economic growth in Africa. Clinton expressed the spirit of this legislation as
follows: "We are going to pay more attention to those who are making
the right political and economic reforms. We want to help the magnets
of change. Sub-Saharan Africa is still a largely untapped market of 600
to 700 million people" (Scholz 1995:23). With the assistance of the IMF
and the World Bank, most of the poor countries in Africa were forced to
implement the economic policies know as Structural Adjustment Programs (ESAP) which required poor countries in sub-Saharan Africa to

cut back on social welfare and privatise parastatals (government-owned companies) as well as allow capital mobility. Obviously, to fulfil such policies required poor countries to sacrifice their already poor citizens. In this way, the USA, through the assistance of the multilateral monetary institutions such as the IMF and World Bank, has actually furthered its imperial greed among the global poor. They have created a situation whereby wealth in the poor countries that have implemented neoliberal capitalism, especially in sub-Saharan Africa, gets over-accumulated by a few to the exclusion of the majority of the citizens, who are reduced to abject poverty.

The USA's self-proclaimed image as a paragon of global morality is usually driven by impulses of economic greed. The most proclaimed or foreign-funded projects such as civil societies and democratic governance in sub-Saharan Africa are not aimed at improving the lives of the majority of the poor citizens in this part of world, but to enable its companies to have access to the natural resources from these countries. The history of American imperialism in sub-Saharan Africa shows that the USA is not much concerned with democratic good governance. One finds that ruthless and oppressive dictators were never rebuked as long as they supported the USA's economic interests. The following chapter will attempt to show how this type of greed is inseparable from capitalism and that it is the main cause of our human suffering.

Chapter 3

Greed as a Sign of Corrupted Human Nature

Greed remains one of the greatest problems of human existence. The question that we have failed to answer is: why are we so greedy? It seems almost ingrained within human nature to be discontent with the material things we already have. At the same time, to be told that we are greedy can be disconcerting and make us feel debased, since greed evokes images of vulgarity and indecency. The reason for this is that greed is an expression of our innate human failure to set limits, to be content, and also to acknowledge that others need the same goods that we enjoy. Someone who keeps eating past the point of satiation is likely to be physically sick. In the same way, greed is usually destructive to the common good. Put simply, greed implies acting in a way that ultimately deprives others of a decent livelihood. Usually, a greedy person shows compulsiveness. The inherent human impulse of wanting to hoard as much wealth as possible to oneself defies the existence of any grain of empathy or compassion towards others. As a result, it incites quarrels and wars. Almost all human suffering and injustice can be traced back to this dark characteristic of human nature.

In traditional Greek thought, greed was considered to be in contrast with the concept of *euthymia*, which denoted a life in accordance with the principles of harmony, moderation and a cautious pursuit of pleasure. For example, Democritus (460–396 BC) condemned greed:

> "Euthymia *arises for men from moderation* (metriotes) *of pleasure and harmonious* (symmetria) *of life. Things in excess or deficiency are apt to change and create disturbances (movements) in the soul. But souls moved by great divergences* (diastemata), *are not stable, nor do they have* euthymia... *If you no longer desire more [than you have], you cease to suffer in your soul."*
> *(Cited in Nill 1985:77)*

This suggests that an unchecked obsession or lust for wealth is antithetical to euthymia.

Greed is connected with our human consumption habits such as over-eating and usually results in physical suffering. In some instances, such suffering finds alleviation in vomiting. However, since greed is an impulse, it has the capability of inhibiting one's reflective faculties. In this way, the greedy person becomes an addict; he or she compulsively repeats these consumption habits over and over again, becoming trapped in a vicious cycle. Democritus illustrates this as follows:

> "All who derive their pleasures from the stomach, exceeding (hyperballein) what is fitting in eating, drinking, or sexual activity have pleasures that are brief and short-lived. For this desire is always present for the same things, and when people get what they desire, the pleasure passes quickly, and they have nothing good for themselves except a brief enjoyment and then again the need for the same things returns." (Nill 1985:78)

In the above citation, eating or consumption habits that are taken into extremes without setting limits is shown as some form of mental imbalance. For this reason, Democritus cautioned that "striving after possessions and wealth, if not limited by sufficiency, is far more painful than extreme poverty, for greater desires make for greater needs *(endeiai)*" (Nill 1985:78). For Democritus, greed is a subjective state whereby the individual's desires take precedence over needs. When an individual's desires overcome a person's capability to know what is sufficient, they can be driven to the extent where the only thing that matters is the fulfilment of these desires, even at the cost of losing wealth. A greedy person's state of existence can thus be far more painful than that of a poor person, as there is an inherent imbalance between desires and needs for the former. Democritus went on to characterise such a state of existence as rooted in ignorance or irrationality, and suggested that greed can be viewed as incommensurable with wisdom. Nill further elaborates that "fame and wealth without intelligence are dangerous passions" (Nill 1985:80). What this suggests is that wealth without wisdom can become lethal, as those riches cannot be appropriately managed. Wisdom was thus of utmost importance for the ancient Greeks in order to control inordinate desires for material things that are usually triggered by greed.

In Latin, the word *avaritia* is used interchangeably with greed. In *The Shorter Oxford English Dictionary*, avarice is defined as an "inordinate desire of getting and hoarding wealth". In the same dictionary the word 'inordinate' is defined as an existential human condition that is "not ordered; irregular, disorderly; not controlled or restrained. Not kept within orderly limits, immoderate, excessive. Not conforming or subject to law or order, disorderly; immoderate, intemperate". All of these adjectives stress the idea that avaritia or greed is the antithesis of a well-ordered life and is a perversion of the norm, in that it creates disorderliness in the character of the individual.

In the Middle Ages, the Church condemned avarice or greed as an expression of a fallen human nature. To counter greed, the main teaching of the Church Fathers was that wealth accumulated should be shared with those who were poor. Another way of tackling greed was by the rejection of usury (making a profit from trade or money given on credit). The condemnation of usury was based on the rationale that those who borrow money are usually poor; hence, to charge an interest on their borrowing was to exert an extra burden on those already deprived. Usury meant charging a price that was excessively higher than what the product cost for its production. Equally, a monopolist who controlled people's economic activities in order to take advantage of their necessities was regarded as committing a sin of usury (Tawney 1926:48–50; Viner 1978:85–90). However, it needs to be said that the Medieval Church did not condemn trading—only the greed that was prevalent within it. During the Reformation era, the same condemnation of avarice exists in the writings of the reformers. For example, Martin Luther was very uncompromising in his teaching against greed and usury, as outlined in the following statement:

> "When once the rogue's eye and greedy belly of a merchant find that people must have his wares, or that the buyer is poor and needs them, he takes advantage of him and raises the price. Because of his avarice, therefore, the goods must be priced as much higher as the greater need of other fellows will allow, so that the neighbor's need becomes as it were the measure of the goods' worth and value." (Luther 1962:248)

In the above quotation, we can deduce that when economic relations are guided by the spirit of greed they become abusive and harmful to those involved. This is because an avaricious person is primarily concerned with his or her own self-interest without any sense of concern for the wellbeing of the other person with whom they are dealing.

With the evolution of modern capitalism in the Western world, the term greed has been euphemistically replaced with the word 'self-interest'. This approach to human nature and human economic relations was more pragmatic. An era which heralded this type of thinking is usually referred to as the 'Age of Enlightenment'. The previous ecclesiastical economic ethic which condemned avarice in economic affairs was abandoned on the basis that such a teaching was rather myopic about human nature. From both the political and the economic front, one finds the evolution of a concerted epistemic effort whereby Western scholars argued that there was a symbiotic relationship between political and economic liberalism.

On Greed, Political and Economic Liberalism and the Justification of Dehumanisation

Political and economic liberalism justified greed as indispensable to wealth creation and the ruling of a country. From a political perspective, the English philosopher David Hume wrote an essay titled *On the Independency of Parliament* in which he said:

> "... in contriving any system of government, and fixing the several checks and controls of the constitution, every man [sic] ought to be supposed a knave, *and to have no other end, in all his actions, than private interest. By this interest we must govern him, notwithstanding his insatiable avarice and ambition, co-operate to the public good. It is therefore, a just* political *maxim*, that every man must be supposed a knave." [His emphasis] (Hume 1882:117–118)

Such a characterisation of human nature as knavish was a form of dehumanisation. This dehumanisation comes out clearly when one traces the meaning of the word 'knave' which was used by Hume as the primary characteristic of human nature. For example, the *Webster's New Dictionary of Synonyms* states that the word belongs to a family of words such as "villain, scoundrel, blackguard, rascal, rogue, scamp, rapscallion and miscreant", words which suggest "a reprehensible person utterly lacking in principles". Worthlessness, meanness and unscrupulousness are further used to describe such a person. For Hume, political liberalism was about harnessing these deplorable human passions for noble purposes in a way that would result in the promotion of the common good. Thus, greed was not necessarily regarded as a negative trait. One can easily caricature this way of thinking by saying that those motivated by greed, who were previously condemned by ecclesiastical morality, did not bring negative consequences to the societies in which they lived. In actual fact, these greedy individuals were beneficial to the flourishing of the common good, even if it was not their motive.

The idea that greedy individuals were beneficial to the flourishing of the common good in society seems to have been integral to the ascendancy of liberal capitalism in Western societies. Adam Smith is usually accredited as being the father and founder of liberal capitalism with the idea that greed is at the heart of the working of the economy. Our human economic relations should be understood as feasting on each other's greed. In Bernard de Mandeville's parody, *The Fable of the Bees*, he poetically emphasised the prevalence of greed in the liberal economy as follows:

> *Vast numbers thronged that fruitful Hive;*
> *Yet those Numbers made 'em thrive*
> *Millions endeavoring to supply*
> *Each other's Lust and Vanity*
> *While other Millions were employed,*
> *Thus, every part was full of Vice*
> *(Mandeville 1988:18–36)*

In Mandeville's parody, it was the vices of the bees within the hive that enabled the bees to enjoy a prosperous life. But he also went on to show how this prosperity was severely diminished over the passage of time, when the bees were converted into virtuous citizens. Thus, from this observation he deduced that if vices, luxury and corruption were connected to economic prosperity, then virtue could only lead to economic decay and poverty (Mandeville 1988:34).

For this reason, Mandeville also chided moralists in his poem, *The Moral*, in which he makes it clear that human beings owe their ultimate wellbeing to greed:

> *Fraud, Luxury and Pride must live,*
> *While we the Benefits receive:*

Do we not owe the Growth of Wine
To a dry shabby crooked Vine?
So vice is beneficial found,
Bare virtue can't make nations live
In Splendor.
(Mandeville 1988:36–37)

Here Mandeville acknowledges that although vices such as fraud and corruption can be condemned on a moral basis, they are advantageous for society at large by generating economic success and prosperity. The analogy of wine which we harvest from a 'shabby crooked Vine' sends an unequivocal message to the reader that we are all ultimately beneficiaries of vices, even when they incite our moral indignation. The mistake made by moralists was teaching people about the evils of greed whilst failing to recognise that it was the primary cause for the flourishing of wealth.

Another problem with morality is that it teaches people what *ought* to happen instead of acknowledging what *is* happening. What ought to happen is impractical, whilst what is happening is practical and real. As he puts it, "One of the greatest reasons why so few people understand themselves, is, that most writers are always teaching men [sic] what they should be, and hardly ever trouble their heads with telling them what they really are" (Mandeville 1988:25). For Mandeville, it was a matter of adopting a pragmatist outlook that would be beneficial to human self-understanding. All the edifices of civilization did not arise as a result of self-denial, but through what moralists regarded as moral weaknesses: avarice, vanity, luxuriousness, corruption, ambition and so forth. Whilst these moral weaknesses were private vices, they were upon final analysis public virtues, in the sense that they were good insofar as they were useful to others. For example, a public official who is convicted of corruption or stealing public funds is usually sent to prison. Those who guard prisons would not have guaranteed employment were it not for the vices of such an individual.

Mandeville further emphasised the fragility of morality when he made a claim to the effect that all moral conduct has a selfish basis. Thus, someone who might try to help a person who is in a predicament should be understood as selfish because of the underlying need and concealed intention of satisfying his or her own need for compassion. Even those people who performed acts of self-denial or self-sacrifice were only doing so out of love of praise or fear of blame. Human nature is simply caught up in a vicious circle of self-interest or greed. Our human relations are just an interplay of greed and selfishness. Mandeville writes:

> "*The Greediness we have after the Esteem of others, and the Raptures we enjoy in the Thoughts of being liked, and perhaps admired, are Equivalents that overpay the Conquest of the strongest Passions... All Human Creatures, before they are yet polish'd, receive an extraordinary Pleasure in hearing themselves prais'd: this we are all conscious of, and therefore when we see a Man openly enjoy and feast on this Delight, in which we have no share, it rouses our Selfishness, and immediately we begin to Envy and Hate him. For this reason, the well-bred Man conceals his Joy, and utterly denies that he feels any, and by this means consulting and soothing our Selfishness, he averts that Envy and Hatred.*" (Mandeville 1924:68–78)

For Mandeville, all human emotions and actions have a common source of origin: greed or selfishness. Our human tendency towards generosity is in itself some form of disguised greed or selfishness. A virtuous person is merely someone who is capable of concealing his or selfishness, thus averting the wrath that usually arises from being openly greedy. Following on from this, Mandeville went on to say that greed gives rise to envy and hatred. On the premise that the human being is an egoist, Mandeville developed an economic creed that exonerated the pursuit of selfishness for luxurious purposes. Mandeville may sound like an extreme pragmatist, but his thinking had far-reaching implications for the evolution of economic liberalism. He introduced an element of philosophical realism in human behaviour with specific reference to human economic relations. His main insight in this regard was that we should admit that economic relations are not concerned with virtue, but with vices that were previously condemned by medieval ecclesiastical morality. Through *The Fable of the Bees*, Mandeville articulated the economic theory that came to be known as 'laissez-faire'. The main presumption of this theory is that when individuals are left to pursue their vices, things tend to find their own equilibrium. The other is that the individual's pursuit of his or her vices is actually beneficial to the larger community in the long-run.

Greed and the Common Good

While Mandeville interpreted greed or self-interest as a 'private vice', in the *Wealth of Nations*, Adam Smith substituted 'private vice' with terms such as 'advantage' or 'interest'. A crucial point to note here is Smith's substitution with terms that are much more modest and appealing. The Mandevillian thesis that greed was the main reason for the flourishing of wealth became the basis for Smith's argument that economic relations are about appealing to each other's greed or self-interest (Smith 1976:26–27; Viner 1958:339–340). Smith went further in his claim by suggesting that greed has some form of divine origin. The divine origin of greed was articulated in his earlier book entitled *The Theory of Moral Sentiments*. In this book he states that the rich "consume little more than the poor, and in spite of their *natural selfishness* and rapacity. They divide with the poor the produce of all their improvements." In the process, he alleged that "they are led by the *invisible hand* to make nearly the same distribution of the necessities of life which would have been made had the earth been divided into equal proportions among all its inhabitants; and thus; *without intending it*, advance the interests of society" (Smith 1872:305). Although a business person might be solely driven by greed, Smith justified this on the grounds that this is directed by divine intervention in a way that ultimately leads to socially beneficial ends, albeit unintentional.

The idea that greed was sanctioned by Divine Providence had its early connection with a religious belief in Deism. The Deists believed that the promotion of human happiness depended entirely on God's Providence. What this entailed was that the infinite goodness of God had the capability to provide all creatures with happiness in accordance with their natures (Byrne 1989:53–54). The idea that greed was part and parcel of the working of Providence was stated by Adam Smith in *The Theory of Moral Sentiments*:

> *"The idea of that divine Being, whose benevolence and wisdom have, from all eternity, contrived and conducted the immense machine of the universe, so as at all times to produce the greatest possible quantity of happiness, is certainly of all the objects of human contemplation by far the most sublime... The administration of the greatest system of the universe, however, the care of the universal happiness of all rational and sensible beings, is the business of God and not of man." (Smith 1872:210)*

The above quotation implies that since God created the universe and all its creatures through wisdom and benevolence, it follows that all creatures depend entirely on God's benevolence for their own wellbeing rather than on the benevolence of human beings. This way of thinking allowed Smith to justify greed partly on the basis that with the assistance of Providence, the greed of the rich would not endanger the wellbeing of the poor because "when Providence divided the earth among a few lordly masters, it neither forgot nor abandoned those who seemed to have been left out in the partition. These last, too, enjoy their share of all that it produces" (Smith 1872:163).

According to Smith, everything has been meticulously designed by Providence, in such a way that there is a delicate balance in the working of the economy, and as such there is no need to be concerned with the wellbeing of the poor. As we have seen previously, Smith coined the concept of the 'invisible hand' as partly involved in directing individual greedy impulses for benevolent purposes. This invisible hand has the capability to draw goodness out of private greed (Tawney 1926:51; Cort 1988:11). Greed was part of God's grace to human beings because it enabled the flourishing of the poor in the long-run. Steeped in the same belief, in 1877 an American lawyer by the name of Samuel Tilden gave a speech at a testimonial dinner for the American business tycoon, Julius Morgan, in which he said:

> "You are doubtless in some degree, clinging to the illusion that you are working for yourself, but it is my pleasure to claim that you are working for the public. While you are scheming of your own selfish ends, there is an overruling and wise Providence directing that the most of all you do should inure to the benefit of the people. Men of colossal fortunes are in effect, if not in fact, trustees for the public." (See Canterbury 1987:114)

It is explicitly clear in the above speech that Morgan viewed his greed as being directed by God for social beneficial ends that surpassed all human scheming. In this mode of thought there is no need for planning how the economy should function. This lays out the origins of the neoliberal capitalist ideal in which the government is discouraged from interference in the functioning of the economy. Rooted in this is an implicit belief in the Smithian concept of the invisible hand. There are some scholars who maintained that the concept of the invisible hand implies that though human economic behaviour is accentuated by greed, it gives rise to a spontaneous order in society.

Friedrich von Hayek is one such proponent of this idea. He writes, "the spontaneous collaboration of free men [sic] often creates things which are greater than their individual minds ever fully comprehend... is the great discovery of classical and political economy which has become the basis of our understanding not only of economic life but of most truly social phenomena" (Hayek 1948:8). He went on to say that the individualism that arises from such an understanding would lead us to adopt "an individualism of anti-rationalism" (Hayek 1948:8–9). This 'individualism of anti-rationalism' implies individuals acting and behaving in ways that do not necessarily involve rational planning and systematic execution. According to Hayek, self-interest involves pursuing something which the individual deems desirable and through the free market system, the individual ends up contributing "to ends which were not part of his purpose" (Hayek 1948:15). It is due to the reality of universal ignorance that Hayek was against what he called 'rationalistic individualism', which tends to overlook the fact that individuals are usually required to submit themselves to irrational forces of society (Hayek 1948:20).

Greed as a Violation of Rationalism and the Affirmation of Beastly Passions

Proponents of liberal capitalism made sense of the predominance of greed in economic relations through concepts such as 'the invisible hand', 'vices' and 'spontaneous orders'. All of the aforementioned concepts suggest that greed defies rationality. However, from a humanistic perspective there were scholars who refuted the individualism of anti-rationalism. For example, John Ruskin (1898:39–49) maintained that "men of business do indeed know how they themselves made their money, or how, on occasion, they lost it. Playing a long-practised game, they are familiar with the chances of its cards, and can rightly explain their losses and gain." Ruskin went as far as to say that in playing this game of making money, for business people "the art of becoming rich, in the common sense, is not absolutely nor finally the art of accumulating much money for ourselves, but also of contriving that our neighbours shall have less." In accurate terms, it is "the art of establishing maximum inequality in our favour." This was clearly a vehement refutation of the presumption that greedy people are moved by irrational forces to behave in the way they do.

Contrary to the idea that greed is based on rationalism, other critics of capitalism such as Karl Marx and Friedrich Engels supported the idea that greed is based on anti-rationalism. They suggested that greedy people are pushed by irrational forces by which social existence is reduced to "*war amongst the greedy—competition*" [their italics] (Marx and Engels 1975:270–271). Within this state of greed, human economic relations are reduced to "a state of universal prostitution within the community" whereby individuals relate to each other solely with the expectation of personal gain to be accrued. With the evolution of the bourgeois social class, dehumanisation was carried to heights of magnanimous proportions because, "All that is solid melts into air, all that is holy is profaned, and man is at last compelled to face with sober senses, his real conditions of life, and his relations with his kind" (Marx and Engels 1988:58). In this regard, no relations are regarded as important unless these relations chime with the bourgeoisie's impulses of greed. The same presumption that capitalistic economic relations are based on anti-rationalism was adopted by Thorstein Veblen in *The Theory of the Leisure Class*.

According to Veblen, the leisure class consists of those who own property. The ownership of their property rests on the fact that other people (mainly the lower-class) work for them. For Veblen, the idea of praising prowess and exploitation in ancient societies was the causal factor of the rise of modernist predatory capitalist economic practices. The word 'predatory', used by Veblen to characterise the leisure class or capitalists, shows his conviction that this class is largely driven by instincts rather than rationality. He purports that "the predatory instinct and the consequent approbation of predatory efficiency are deeply ingrained in the habits of thought of those people who have passed under the discipline of a protracted predatory culture" (Veblen 1931:30). Veblen's use of the phrase 'protracted predatory culture' to characterise the capitalists' behaviour is dehumanising; it implies some form of existence in which one's humanity is utterly diminished. However, this predatory habit has no rational explanation besides what Veblen considers a motivation for power and honour through endless accumulation and acquisition of wealth. The appetite for wealth among the leisure class is simply insatiable. The need to acquire more wealth becomes addictive to the extent that it leads to compulsive greed, similar to a chronic illness. He writes:

> "But as fast as a person makes new acquisitions, and becomes accustomed to the resulting new standard of wealth, the new standard forthwith ceases to afford appreciably greater satisfaction as the earlier standard did. The tendency in any case is constantly to make the present pecuniary standard the point of departure for a fresh increase of wealth; and this in turn gives rise to a new standard of sufficiency and a new pecuniary classification of one's self as compared with one's neighbours. So far as concerns the present acquisition, the end sought by accumulation is to rank high in comparison with the rest of the community in point of pecuniary strength." (Veblen 1931:31)

Thus, the element of insatiability dominates the behaviour of the leisure class. Within this state of insatiability what is acquired is never enough; rather, it is a stepping stone for further acquisition. Competition in acquiring material things is set in motion by greed without any recourse to rational justification. The imagery that is coined by Veblen to describe greed is 'chronic dissatisfaction'. He explains, "The normal average individual [among the leisure class] will live in *chronic dissatisfaction* with his present lot" because "when he has reached what may be called the normal pecuniary standard of the community, *chronic dissatisfaction* will give place to a restless straining to place a wider and ever-widening pecuniary interval between himself and this average standard" [my italics] (Veblen 1931:31). Therefore, greed has a psychological explanation in which the acquisition of wealth can be viewed as a type of addiction.

Psychologically, an addiction manifests itself as a type of compulsive behaviour which usually defies rational explanation. It is partly for this reason that those from the leisure class are driven by the desire to emulate the wealth of those who belong to their class, creating an endless economic state of competitive accumulation without any standard for sufficiency. Metaphorically speaking, it is as if the individual is on a perpetual slippery slope. In the process of endless accumulation the individual severs himself from communal belonging. This idea appears more succinctly when Veblen says, "When he enters upon the predatory stage, where self-seeking in the narrower sense becomes the dominant note, this propensity goes with him still, as the pervasive trait that shapes his scheme of life" (Veblen 1931:33).

By living life as a predator, the greedy person sees the purpose of his life in terms of acquisition without rational explanation. The dehumanising aspect of greed has been attributed to the animalistic behaviour inherent in us as a species. For example, the father of social biology, Herbert Spencer, alluded to this idea when he said that a realistic observation of nature shows that among animals in the wild "the stronger often carries off by force the prey which the weaker has caught" (Spencer 1907:13). This was a manifestation of natural law—a law that is fundamental to the natural ordering of reality. Since the law of nature is the bedrock for all that is real, human social arrangements should be ordered in a way that concurs with the law of nature. Spencer would hence give a stern warning against trying to interfere with a social hierarchy in which the strong exploit the weak, as this is rooted in the natural order of the world. He warns, "Any arrangements which in a considerable degree prevent superiority from profiting by the rewards of superiority, or shield inferiority from the evils it entails—are arrangements diametrically opposed to the progress of organizations and the reaching of a higher life" (Spencer 1907:162). This way of thinking suggests that predatory behaviour is not only an expression of superiority but is beneficial to the attainment of a highly evolved social life. A pride of lions that forcefully take carcasses from weaker carnivorous animals in the game reserve are most likely to prosper and flourish.

Some neoliberal economists have gone as far as to say that there are some similarities between the feeding behaviour of wild carnivorous animals and human economic behaviour in the free market. As Stephen Magee maintains, this beastly human nature has some implications in human economic behaviour. He writes:

> "The animal kingdom is a rich laboratory in which to learn economic lessons about complex systems. Biology teaches us that small differences in fitness have enormous effects on survival. Selfish behaviour is the dominant form of animal behaviour. Almost all feeding behaviour within interspecies is selfish. Predators and parasites increase their welfare at the expense of prey and hosts." (Magee 2000:255–258)

What Magee suggests here is that human economic behaviour within a capitalistic free market economic system is comparable to the feeding behaviour of wild animals, whereby feeding on each other greedily leads to the prosperity of one at the expense of the other. Greed, in this regard, is undoubtedly a manifestation of beastly passions in human beings.

According to Magee, this beastly feeding behaviour is also prevalent among human economic relations in the practice of specialization. Through a process of specialization in a particular economic activity, one is guaranteed of averting the wrath of others' greed, as one ends up doing what they know best in such a way that they achieve some competitive advantage over others. It is through the economic theory of comparative advantage of international trade "that nations and individuals do only that which they do best, as such the lessons of economic comparative advantage and of bio economic increasing competition are the same—specialize or die" (Magee 2000:258). The only mechanism for survival within this greed-dominated economic context is to focus one's greed towards a particular specialty. In the context of a beastly feeding frenzy, the instinct of having a whole carcass to oneself drives most of the beasts into a fierce fatal combat.

An observation of feeding habits observed on a National Geographic programme proves the same idea. After a pack of hyenas collaborated in the killing of a kudu in a South African game reserve, they went into a feeding frenzy. However, when they had almost finished devouring the kudu, the queen hyena dragged the remainder of it with her. Those who dared to challenge her were met with a vicious attack which was in some cases fatal. As the leader of this group her greed made her act in a way that explicitly showed that she did not have any sense of care and concern for their welfare. Faced with the possibility of having less food after the feeding frenzy, the queen hyena was overwhelmed by an instinct which caused her to forcefully take the last remains of the carcass for herself. Is this behaviour different from our human economic and political national and international relations? Timothy Radcliffe likened contemporary politics and economics to the beasts in the Darwinian Jungle. He avers:

> "In the Darwinian jungle there can be no forgiveness. The neces-
> sary consequence of weakness and failure is extinction; and it is
> good that this happens, for that is evolution. We human beings
> are the result of a ruthless process which wipes out innumerable
> species because they could not adapt. What is creative of our
> humanity is an unforgiving history. I suspect that the image
> of the survival of the fittest operates in a similar unforgiving
> way in much contemporary economics and politics." (Timothy
> 1994:762)

In the theory of evolution, Charles Darwin (1859) postulated that species which successfully pursue greedy impulses are most likely to succeed in life's struggle for survival. Those who survive are endowed with a particular genetic predisposition that enables them to reproduce their own kind. This came to be known as the principle of 'natural selection'. For Darwin, the greedy are simply expressing or playing out the law of nature which destines them to act as agents of natural selection. A species which fails to pursue its greedy impulses exposes itself to the danger of being wiped out of existence. In this way, greed can be considered vital in advancing the purposes of natural selection. Through their greed, the rich are 'naturally selected' as suitable members for the perpetuation of human existence. Darwin actually believed that the poor and the old were not supposed to be helped because humanitarianism was against the law of natural selection. He stated:

> "With savages, the weak in body are soon eliminated; and those that survive commonly exhibited a vigorous state of health. We civilized men, on the other hand, do our utmost to check the process of elimination; we build asylums for the imbecile, the maimed, and the sick; we institute poor laws; our medical men exert their utmost skill to save the life of every one to the last moment… thus the weak members of civilized societies propagate their kind. No one who has attended to the breeding of domestic animals will doubt that this must be highly injurious to the race of man." (Darwin 1859:185)

It is clear that when someone is motivated by greed they usually lack a sense of care and concern for the wellbeing of others.

We should bear in mind, however, that Darwin's theory of natural selection was partly influenced by Thomas Malthus, who is popularly known as the father of population geography. Malthus' thesis was that if human beings were left unchecked by nature, their tendency to increase themselves could easily outstrip the available means of subsistence. The occurrence of diseases, epidemics, wars, plagues and famine from time to time ensure that human beings do not increase themselves in a way that outstrips the available means of subsistence (Malthus 1958:6; Heilbroner 1972:83). Malthus' admiration of greed extends so far that in his main thesis he observes that the main problem of the world arises from the fact that there are too many people in it. Consequently, it is simply logical that an increase in the sum of humanity entails an increase in poverty. The more human mouths there are to feed, the more pressure is exerted on resources. In such a scenario, Malthus did not believe that the poor should be allowed to exist as their existence made them prone to being nature's suitable candidates for depopulation. 'Welfarism' was dangerous because it enabled the poor to propagate themselves. To those who supported welfarism, he warned, "A poor man may marry with little or no prospect of being able to support a family in independence. They may be said therefore in some measure to create the poor which they maintain" (Malthus 1958:45–50). In this mode of thought we have the naturalisation of greed as a contingent within nature which should not be interrupted through human activities.

Critics of greed in the capitalistic system such as Karl Marx were swift in seeing the motif of the beast in the theories of Malthus and Darwin. In his letter to Engels, Marx protested that "Darwin was applying the Malthusian theory also to plants and animals. It is remarkable how Darwin recognizes among beasts and plants his English society... the Malthusian struggle for existence" (See Knight 1991:51). The idea of connecting greed to the life of a beast was also echoed by Engels in his *The Dialectics of Nature* when he retorted that "Darwin did not know what a bitter satire he wrote on mankind, when he showed that free competition, the struggle for existence... is the normal state of the animal kingdom" (Knight 1991:51–52). Marx and Engels were thus staunchly against the Malthusian and Darwinian idea of naturalising greed by transferring it from human existence into the realm of nature.

Some biologists have traversed their materialistic analysis of human bodily functioning and tried to explain the existence of greed in human behaviour in terms of genes. Richard Dawkins provides a natural explanation of greed as something encoded in our genes. For Dawkins, the real unit of natural selection is the gene. This gene itself is greedy and habitually uses our bodies for purposes that serve selfish ends. Robertson pertinently remarks: "This is an image borrowed from Smithian economics, and it carries with it a similar false assurance that if genes are left properly to their own self-interested devices, all will be for the best in the best of all possible worlds" (Robertson 2001:69). Genes that propel us to be greedy enable us to succeed more than those that compel us to be altruistic. Peter Singer caricatured this way of thinking as follows:

77

> "*Modern human beings are the outcome of a long and unceasing evolutionary struggle. In that struggle, some individuals succeed in feeding themselves and surviving long enough to reproduce. Others do not. Those who succeed pass their genes to the next generation, the genes of those who lose are extinguished from the population. Egoists who act first and foremost in their own interests stand a better chance of winning than altruists, who put helping others to win ahead of maximizing their own chances of winning. Since traits like selfishness are at least in part determined by our genes, this means that the number of egoists will grow and the number of altruists will shrink. In the long-run and evolution has already had a very long run indeed—there will be no true altruists at all.*" (Singer 1995:85–86)

In this way of thinking, the presumption is that greed guarantees success in human existence. The main reason for this is that greed is encoded in the nature of the greedy person and this gene is passed on from one generation to another without any interruption. This attempt to biologically prove the origins of greed is evidently captured in the thinking of Howard Margolis (Margolis 1982:26–28) who stated, "self-interested creatures, other things being equal, will be able to leave more descendants carrying their genes than would non-self-interested creatures. Hence natural selection will favour self-interest." Equally, a group that is solely greedy for its own group "will have a selection advantage over other groups deficient in that propensity", which follows that "within a group, self-interest will be favoured and among groups, group interest will be favoured."

Inferentially, greed has a selection advantage in two ways. Firstly, a greedy individual within a community will prosper more than one who cares for the wellbeing of the community at large. Secondly, a nation or an ethnic group that is greedy in relation to others will be favoured by natural selection over one that is generous. In the light of this 'biologisation' of greed, an impression is created to the effect that as humans we are driven to act in a greedy manner because of our predetermined biological make-up. The assurance here is that greed is our natural biological predisposition. A question that has been raised by many scholars is whether genes are rational entities. But the idea that greed is part and parcel of our natural impulse implies that as humans we are driven to always act in a greedy manner. The other implication of this 'biologisation' of greed is that greed is addictive to the extent that it defines an individual's character throughout his or her life. However, neoliberal economists maintain that greed has a rational explanation in the working of economics.

Greed and Utility Maximization

Gordon Tullock and Richard McKenzie stated, "The rational individual, in search of a spouse, will attempt to maximize utility as in all other endeavours. This means that he will seek to minimize the cost incurred through marriage and family" (1985:79). The implication of this is that through the application of rationality, greed helps us to avoid relationships that have the potential to jeopardise our fortunes. Since individuals are presumed to always be driven by passions of greed, they are expected to only act after calculating the costs and benefits to be accrued in a love affair. Thus, all actions are considered rational when they lead to the maximization of utility, and the only plausible way of achieving this maximization is through greed. Utility maximization therefore becomes a rational explanation for greed. The same type of thinking can be discerned from the ideas of Alan Hamlin (1986:16–17) who characterised modern economic rationality as "ends rationality", which is based on the presumption that the individual acts solely with the aim of maximizing utility. The main belief here is that "all interests are commensurable into a single dimension—utility—so that in choosing among actions the individual needs only to compare utility content of the alternative." In this way of thinking we are led to believe that all people make individual choices with the sole aim of maximizing utility. This is likewise the main goal of economic activities.

Hamlin (1986:17–36) went on to postulate that among some of the characteristics of the ends-rational view of utility maximization is that "it is personal in the sense that the utility to be maximized is my own. Other individuals do not enter into the evaluation process... I am concerned about you only to the extent that my utility is involved." The implication of this utility maximization is that the individual, who is a unit of utility maximization, should not be subsumed under the collective nature of society. One is thus expected to associate with others solely on the basis of maximizing one's utility. Whether the maximization of one's utility deprives others of their own livelihoods becomes something that is factored into consideration. Hamlin went on to say that even an economic act of giving produces utility. Here we are led to believe that altruism has its origins in utility maximization. He avers, "Whilst altruism may appear to be un-self-interested in the short-run, its long-term benefits—including the benefits of living in a society of altruists—may dominate these short-run costs even in the egoist's private calculus." If individuals are single-mindedly fixated on attaining utility maximization, they are more likely to use an altruistic relation for purposes that help them achieve this. The underlying basis of this theory, therefore, is the assumption that all human beings are greedy.

But can utility maximization come to a point where it reaches satiation? Modern economics suggests that this utility sometimes diminishes after the consumption of a particular product, as one can end up losing interest in that product and replace it with another. For this reason, utility maximization implies that as human beings we exist in a perennial, subjective state of insatiability.

Utility maximization demands that people should always act solely on the basis of promoting one's self-interest; hence, it discounts the reality of human satisfaction through socialisation. People are presumed to act only after calculating costs and benefits. For example, Paul Heyne

(1983:272–283) advised that, "Government is people interacting, paying attention to the expected costs and benefits of the alternatives that they perceive." This idea implies that an action which is ultimately beneficial is one which derives more, as that which is huge is preferable to that which is small. We can only manage to attain that which is huge by depriving others through a process of accumulating more and more for ourselves at the expense of others. Heyne went on to say that "economic theory assumes that people act in their own interest, not that they act in the public interest." It is clear that that which belongs to the public is not favoured because it compromises our opportunity to maximize our individual utility. This can be deduced from the belief that all human beings are rational to the extent that they always apply reason whenever they make choices, yet these choices are only rational when they help us to promote our greed or utility maximization.

The rationalisation of greed through the theory of utility maximization is also found among game theorists. For example, Robert Axelrod advanced a game theory of cooperation in which he said that cooperation among greedy people is possible. He maintained that "the assumption of self-interest is really just an assumption that concern for others does not completely solve the problem of when to cooperate with them and when not to" (Axelrod 1984:6–7). Here we are assured that self-interest or greed dictates when we should cooperate with others or refrain from doing so. According to Axelrod, since cooperation is mostly based on the principle of 'tit for tat', it equally follows that "cooperation can indeed emerge in a world of egoists without central authority" (Axelrod 1984:20). In short, the purpose of cooperation among greedy people is to maximize their utilities. This way of thinking discounts any grain of pre-commitment to moral values. In this vein, Gordon Tullock and Richard Mackenzie provide a more nuanced view when they say:

> "Economics is not so much concerned with what should be or how individuals should behave, as it is with understanding why people behave the way they do. Accordingly, our analysis is devoid

(as much as possible) of our own personal values... Therefore, in the context of our analysis, the services of a prostitute are treated no differently than the services of the butcher; they are neither good nor bad—they exist and are subject to analysis. Criminal activity is considered in manner similar to that of legitimate enterprise..." (Tullock and Mackenzie 1985:7)

The main concern of economic analysis is not the moral predisposition of the individual; rather, the focus is on the amount of utility that can be derived from a given economic transaction. However, one would expect that since economics concerns our survival and ultimate wellbeing, there has to be some type of regulation of individual behaviour with regards to what is morally acceptable. The problem that has been associated with this way of thinking is an attempt by economists to portray this humanistic discipline as a natural science where mathematics and graphic representations demonstrate the workings of greed or utility maximization in a quantitative fashion. In this way, emphasis is put on rationality as the main thrust of economics as a discipline. Paul Heyne reiterates this economic commitment to science by saying, "Only individual persons choose" and "people chose rationally, all interactions among choices can be viewed as market processes". In this process of choosing, there is a rational assumption based on the belief that there are "substitutes everywhere" (Heyne 1983:249). The idea that there are 'substitutes everywhere' implies that human greed will never deplete terrestrially finite resources. Here we are being assured that there are no limits to what the individual can acquire because the resources of the earth are inexhaustible. This is another way of rationalising greed, whereby one postulates a situation of inexhaustibility as a permanent reality.

Another attempt at rationalising greed is to argue that greed has nothing to do with morality or that it is morally neutral. It is argued that greed does not necessary lead us to exterminate each other; rather, it enables us to cooperate with each other. Philip Wicksteed's approach was more nuanced when he said, "Our relations with others enter into a system of mutual adjustment by which we further each other's purposes simply as an indirect way of furthering our own" (Wicksteed 1946:166). The issue of the irrelevance of ethical considerations in economic relations is further reinforced by Wicksteed. "The economic relation, then, or business nexus, is necessarily alike for carrying on the life of the peasant and the prince, the saint and the sinner, of the apostle and the shepherd, of the most altruistic and the most egoistic of men" (Wicksteed 1946:171). In this mode of thought, economic relations have nothing to do with morality. The question of whether people are greedy or altruistic is completely irrelevant because economic relations are presumed economic when they are ethically neutral, in that they do not entertain ethical evaluations or considerations. In economic relations, it does not matter whether the other person is "selfish or unselfish" because "each party to an economic relation enters it in the furtherance of his own purposes, not those of the other" (Wicksteed 1946:171–174).

The whole moral evaluation of capitalistic economic relations as a manifestation of greed is to misuse the word 'greed', because a person who is involved in an economic relation should be seen and understood metaphorically as "a man who is playing a game of chess or cricket. He is considering nothing except his game. It would be absurd to call a man selfish for protecting his king in a game of chess, or to say that he was actuated by purely egoistic motives in so doing" (Wicksteed 1946:180). Moral sentiments such as generosity, pity, sympathy and magnanimity are inapplicable when put into a context where business relations are a game. What this way of thinking suggests is that what we regard as greed in economic relations is not greed at all, but a type of behaviour that is simply expected in business relations.

Wicksteed cautioned that moralists have to bear in mind that, "The catholicity of the economic relation extends far enough in either direction to embrace both heaven and hell, and to suggest to each that its own ends may be best served by an ad interim devotion to those of the other would be misleading" (Wicksteed 1946:184). This type of thinking should be seen as another way whereby liberal economists have attempted to absolve greed of its negative connotations and consequences, and to exorcise morality from human economic relations. This attempt relies on the idea of value neutrality, which in turn is based on the subjective theory of value. According to this theory, human economic relations are understood as an expression of preferences on the part of the individual subject in relation to the satisfaction which the individual is expected to derive from the incremental use of goods (See Schumpeter 1986:659–681; Sen 1987:45–47). It is based on an individualistic understanding of a person as endowed with his or her intrinsic properties that cannot be subsumed under the generality of existence. In this respect, what an individual does is subjective or intrinsic to the individual, and there is no way for greed to be subjected to moral scrutiny. Moreover, this subjective theory of value has also come to dominate modern political theory, with reference to political international relations.

Sanitization of Greed in Political International Relations

'National interest' is a word that has been commonly used by scholars and practitioners of politics to substitute the word 'greed'. The ascendancy of political liberalism in Western society was partly based on the presumption that human beings were greedy and a sensible ruler was to take this into consideration upon assumption to political power. This carried a denigrating outlook towards human nature. The rise of political liberalism was also entrenched in the idea that human nature was evil.

Niccole Machiavelli argued in his book *The Prince* that it is within the prerogative of the ruler to indulge in acts of cruelty without resorting to feelings of guilt regarding the treatment of his subjects. According to Machiavelli, a ruler would perish if he or she was always good and should therefore be both cunning and fierce. He admonishes:

> *"A prudent ruler cannot, and must not, honour his word when it places him at a disadvantage and when the reasons for which he*

made his promise no longer exist. If all men were good, this pre-
cept would not be good; but because men are wretched creatures
who would not keep their word to you, you need not keep your
word to them." (Machiavelli 1961:100)

The implication of the above quotation is that rulers should only honour their word when they are fully aware that they are going to gain from such a gesture. What makes human nature so evil is the fact that they are severely self-interested or greedy. It is therefore simply logical that a wise ruler should rule his or her people in terms of protecting their own interests by whatever means necessary. For a Machiavellian ruler, prudence involves being able to commit acts of brutality against subjects.

However, this presumption about human nature was not only found in Western societies, but can also be found in the writings of Confucians in ancient China. For example, Confucian Xun Zi argued against Mencius, who stated that people can do good by returning to their original nature, which is characterised by harmony and tranquillity. Xun Zi rebutted Mencius by insisting that "the nature of man is evil; his goodness is the result of his activity. Now, man's inborn nature is to seek for gain. If this tendency is followed, strife and rapacity result and deference and compliance disappear... Therefore, the sages of antiquity, knowing that man's nature is evil, that it is unbalanced and incorrect... established the authority of rulers to govern the people..." (Cited in Chan 1963:128–131). For Xun Zi, human nature was evil because of its innate tendency towards self-interest.

The same grim outlook towards human nature is echoed by Thomas Hobbes. According to Hobbes, human social cooperation is the result of our human tendency to be greedy and to restrain our greed through reason. To avoid a situation of total mutual destruction, human beings entered social existence on the basis of a contract. Prior to this, human existence was characterised by a festivity of universal war. In their original natural state of existence, human beings are "in that state which is called war, and such a war is of every man against every man, consequently, the life of man solitary, poor, nasty, brutish and short" (Hobbes 1962:98–100). Whilst Hobbes does not tell us directly whether it is within human nature to be greedy, greed is rather implied when he portrays human nature as naturally self-interested. The principle causes of social strife in the state of nature, i.e. "competition, difference and glory" necessitated the existence of a political authority. Hobbes therefore maintains:

> "... the laws of nature—such as justice, equality, modesty, mercy, and, in sum, doing to others as we would be done to—of themselves, without the terror of some power to cause them to be observed, are contrary to our natural passions that carry us to partiality, pride, revenge, and the like. And covenants without the sword are words, and of no strength to secure man at all. Therefore, notwithstanding the laws of nature... if there be no power erected or not great enough for our security, every man will—and lawfully—rely on his own strength and art for caution for all other men." (Hobbes 1962:99)

Thus in the natural state of man, there is no sense of morality. Here the implication is that morality is just an artifice or something which the ruler has to enforce through the application of brutal force. In its natural state, humanity existed without any sense of feeling for fellow men; only the pursuit of individual interest by whatever means. Put simply, Hobbes believed that as human beings we are inhabited by ferocious destructive emotions of all kinds.

For this reason, Robertson asserted, "Hobbes brought us as close as we may ever have come to an integrated scholarly theory of greed" (Robertson 2001:50). Such an observation tells us that Hobbes advanced the idea of human nature being made in such a way that it has no propensity for restraint. In a similar fashion, greed tends to surpass any sense of moral restraint. What makes existence under the government and moral laws an artifice is the reality of the uncontrollable passions within human beings.

As mentioned previously, David Hume was of the conviction that vicious passions can actually be harnessed for something beneficial to the whole of society. Greed is one such passion that could be used for the political and economic wellbeing of society. For Hume, political liberalism is actually about harnessing individual vicious passions (such as greed) for the ruling of a liberal society. In his essay *On the Independence of Parliament*, Hume stated that the liberal constitution should be based on the premise that human beings are knaves, who are presumed to have 'insatiable avarice and ambition', which should be harnessed for the advancement of the common good. Hence, vicious characteristics in a human being are necessary for liberal parliamentary democracy in which there are checks and balances in light of different interests.

However, he cautioned, "If, on the contrary, separate interest be not checked, and be not directed to the public, we ought to look for nothing but faction, disorder, and tyranny from such government" (Hume 1882:119). What this observation implies is that the government within a liberal society has the responsibility to co-ordinate potentially conflicting interests. Failure to do so will only result in social strife and anarchy. Here we need to bear in mind that the term 'separate interests' implies the reality of people being greedy for different as well as for the same things. Within such a presumption, greed could be used in such a way that it actually controls itself.

In his other work, Hume expressed the same idea with reference to private property:

> "It is certain, that no affection of the human mind has both a sufficient force, and a proper direction to counterbalance the love of gain, and render men fit members of society, by making them abstain from the possessions of others. Benevolence to strangers is too weak for this purpose; and as to the other passions, they rather inflame this activity, when we observe, that the larger our possessions are, the more ability we have of gratifying all our appetites. There is no passion, therefore, capable of controlling

the interested affection, but the very affection itself, by an alter-
ation of its direction. Now this alteration must necessarily take
place upon the least reflection; since it is evident, that the passion
is much better satisfied by its restraint, than by its liberty, and
that in preserving society, we make much greater advances in the
acquiring of possessions... The question, therefore, concerning
the wickedness or goodness of human nature, enters not in the
least into that other question concerning the origin of society...
For whether the passion of self-interest be esteemed vicious or
virtuous, it is all a case; since itself alone restrains it; so that if it
be virtuous, men become social by their virtue; if vicious, their
vice has the same effect." (Hume 1972:222–223)

In the above quotation, we are told that self-interest can be self-assuring. Self-interest has the capacity to lead us into behaving constructively, especially when it is in our best interest. The trait that is integral for the flourishing of humanity is the passion of greed. However, what is equally critical to observe is that it is being rationalised as 'the love of gain'. In this rationalisation, it is no longer something which should be judged as morally repulsive. In actual fact, for Hume, greed carries with it some scientific objective purposes in the ordering of society. As we have seen previously, in the ascendancy of modern capitalism in Western societies, greed has become the rational explanation for economic prosperity and social advancement.

Chapter 4

The African Mystification of Greed

The Nigerian 'Nollywood' film industry is brimming with movies that have a common motif of individuals becoming wealthy after entering into a covenant with the underworld. Men who were previously destitute end up becoming billionaires after agreeing to sacrifice their loved ones to the 'cults of the underworld'. In some movies, it is only after the wealth-seeking individual has killed his wife and children that he is miraculously showered with an abundance of wealth from the underworld. Often the wealth begotten through such a covenant is not supposed to be shared with the destitute lest the wealth ends up vanishing into oblivion; in fact, this often has to be given as a vow. This is sometimes even the case when the person is pressed by relatives for material assistance. The individual would rather beg for assistance from others than give from the newly acquired wealth. These movies about wealth are not entirely based on fictitious and artistic imaginations. Rather, they have an element of human experience and show how greed can plunge people into amorality. These stories reflect the human being's insatiable desire to accumulate as much wealth as possible, even when this behaviour defies rationality.

As children, we were warned about the danger of befriending strangers who drive cars and offer to give us a ride. The most terrifying aspect behind this warning was a story of how some children, abducted by a stranger, were found dead with their body parts (such as their hands and heart) missing from their lifeless bodies. Witch doctors advised that those who aspire to become successful business people and attract customers need to obtain the heart of a child. Since children have many years ahead of them, having the heart of a child buried under one's business premises was considered to provide a long lifespan to the business. Any individual who therefore ran a successful business was suspected of using witchcraft, which easily provided an explanation for the abundance of an individual's wealth. Possessing the hand of a child was understood to attract the attention of customers for many years to come.

Many 'murders for *muthi*' (murders committed by business aspirants to harvest body parts) have been reported in various African countries. For example, in South Africa it was once reported in a newspaper that a black business woman who owned a *shebeen* (a business that sells alcohol) was found with a dead white man's hand hidden under the counter. The explanation she gave was that she used the hand to invite customers to her business. How this business woman got hold of the dead white man's hand remained unexplained. The only probable explanation is that the practice was advised by a witch doctor as part of a mystical solution to ensure continued success of her business.

In Zulu, this practice is known as *ukuthwala*, whereby a business person performs some rituals with the assistance of a witch doctor under the belief that such an undertaking will make one's business more prosperous and increase their wealth. Such rituals require human blood, which is usually given to a *tokoloshe* (goblin). These goblins are believed to be human beings that have magically transformed into small creatures; they cannot be seen by the naked eye and are employed as invisible labourers for one's business. Just as the business person who employs tokoloshes has a desire to accumulate as much wealth as possible, the tokoloshes are equally believed to have an insatiable appetite for human blood. Over time, because of their greed for blood, these tokoloshes end up ruining the business of their owner. Sometimes they are also believed to perform underhand dealings such as invisibly ruining the businesses of competitors and luring customers in favour of their owner's business. They are usually considered to be ruthless when it comes to guarding the business interests of their owner.

Among the Shona people of Zimbabwe, these mystical creatures are known as *zvikwambo*. They are usually acquired from witch doctors and are understood to be endowed with powers to maximize one's wealth at the expense of fellow business competitors. In return for their services, zvikwambo are said to demand animal blood for their sustenance. Similar to the tokoloshes, as the business flourishes as a result of their assistance, so does their exponential demand for more and more blood. A business person is required to slaughter an animal so that these zvikwambo can feed on the blood in return for their services. However, these creatures are said to have an insatiable appetite for blood to the extent that one animal cannot satisfy them easily. Because of this, they end up devouring their owner's entire cattle herd. Sometimes these mystical creatures obliterate the business empire which they have helped to build for many years within an unimaginable short space period of time. When the business empire is gone, zvikwambo are believed to turn to the children and relatives of the business owner in pursuit of their unquenchable thirst for blood. Zvikwambo are the ultimate manifestation of mystified greed. The insatiable appetite for blood usually results in the demise of the business and many deaths among the members of the community in which the business is situated.

In traditional African culture, greed is conceptually understood as synonymous with a force of destruction to our common human belonging. It is partly because of the predominance of greed in modern capitalism that this economic system has never been fully appropriated in the African context. Greed is detested as a contributory factor to communal disharmony and as a virulent portent of evil. Here the goodness of the individual is predicated on his or her ability to promote communal well-being. This claim can be authenticated by the fact that post-colonial economic policies were mainly inspired by the urge to promote communal wellbeing rather than promoting the free reign of individual greed. But could it possible that the traditional detest for greed in Africa has been a contributory factor to the continent's failure in appropriating modern capitalism? If greed is causally related to the ascendancy of modern capitalism in the Western world, would it not be reasonable to say that in societies where greed is detested, capitalism cannot succeed?

Greed and Traditional African Economic Behaviour

The economic historian Karl Polanyi made an anthropological comparative observation in which he said that liberal capitalism was relative to the evolution of modern capitalism in the history of Western civilization. Polanyi maintained that before the advent of capitalism, "the individual in primitive society is not threatened by starvation unless the community as a whole is in like predicament. Under the *kraal*-land system of the Kiffirs [sic], for example, destitution is impossible: whoever needs assistance receives it unquestioningly" (Polanyi 1968:163). From this observation, we can deduce that greed is not culturally universal.

Polanyi's insight is affirmed by some pre-colonial Portuguese traders who were trading in cloth and beads in the Zambezi valley in the 14th century. Portuguese traders such as Diego and de Couto recorded in their diaries that the Africans "are lazy to the extent that they will stop as soon as they find enough gold to buy two pieces of cloth to dress themselves, they have neither eagerness or greed as they always rest content with but little" (Cited in Mudenge 1988:27). Here the implication is that African traditional economic relations were mainly based on subsistence and a sense of contentment with that which was deemed sufficient for one's survival. Within such a social setting, over-accumulation of material things would have likely been considered a manifestation of a spirit of greed. Polanyi went on to assert that greed was only introduced to the Africans during the colonial era. He says: "Ironically, the white man's initial contribution to the black man's [sic] world mainly consist-ed in introducing him to the uses of the scourge of hunger. Thus, the colonialist may decide to cut the breadfruit trees down in order to create an artificial food scarcity or may impose a hut tax on the native to force him to batter away his labour" (Polanyi 1968:164). In light of the above quotation, Africans were unfamiliar with the idea of economic relations based on greed.

A practical way of engendering greed in a culture that was based on living according to the principle of sufficiency was to create an economic situation of scarcity. Colonial administrative systems such as that of a hut tax were obviously aimed at creating a situation of demand among Africans which only the colonial system was able to fulfil. In this process, the Africans were sucked into an economic system that was based on greed as a mechanism for self-preservation. Through a series of categories of taxes, Africans were forced to sell their labour to colonial industrial establishments such as mines, farms and manufacturing industries. As a result, the economic principle of sufficiency which had traditionally regulated African traditional economic relations was undermined to the core. For example, H. S. Keigwin, one of the early colonial adminis-trators of Rhodesia, reinforced the idea that Africans were supposed to be exposed to artificial economic forces as a means of forcing them to participate in the colonial economic system. He avers, "The native is conservative, averse to innovations, ignorant of any such thing as the force of economic pressure. Left to themselves, they will not think of any danger till it is on them" (Keigwin 1923:27). This 'force of economic pressure' could only involve manipulating people in a way that would compel them to enter into economic relations of greed.

The traditional condemnation of greed in Africa was usually based on the grounds that it would lead to the deprivation of material wellbeing to other members of the community. Greed had strong links to witch-craft, as can be seen in how greed was facilitated through occult rituals in some African societies. This conceptualisation of greed was alluded to by Jomo Kenyatta when he said, "The selfish or self-regarding man has no name of reputation in the Gikuyu community. An individualist is frowned upon with suspicion and is given the nickname '*mwebongia*', meaning one who works for himself and is likely to end up a wizard... Religious sanction works against him, too, for Gikuyu religion is always on the side of solidarity" (Kenyatta 1953:199).

Greed and Witchcraft

Being a witch or a wizard implies a type of existence that oppos-es communal harmony and solidarity. In African traditional wisdom, witches were believed to have an acute propensity for devouring human flesh. The anthropologist Alexander Robertson claims that there is a con-nection between greed and witchcraft. He writes:

> *"The witch is adept at breaking the 'normal' connections be-tween motives and actions, and reassembling them in reverse ways. A malicious feeling may be translated into physical harm without any observable action. The problem for the moral ma-jority is how to make sense of this. No matter how vigorously you torment your suspects, they are unlikely to give a coherent explanation, ultimately because witches operate with a sort of 'anti-knowledge'." (Robertson 2001:95)*

Robertson's description of a witch echoes the liberal economic idea of greed operating under the principle of anti-rationalism. In African cul-ture, the aspect of anti-rationalism inherent in witchcraft is that it is usu-ally presumed to work under the influence of possession by evil spirits or *mashavi*—a Shona word for alien or evil spirits. For this reason, when a witch acts under the influence of a *shavi*, he or she confesses during a normal state that they were unaware of their actions and were acting out of some external force of compulsion. Thus, in these states of being, there is no coherence between motives and actions. This idea is emphasised in a Shona proverb which says, '*Muroyi haana mugoni*', meaning 'there is no one who can exactly know what the witch is up to'. In the absence of prior knowledge of motives, human actions are susceptible to mutual deception as malice and benevolence are conflated in the same act, thus defying common knowledge.

In another adage about witchcraft, Shona people say, '*Muroyi royera kure kuti vepedyo vakureverere*', the literal translation of which is 'if you are a witch you should practise your witchcraft far away so that neighbours can come to your defence when you are accused of witchcraft'. Since witchcraft is irreconcilable with moral values, the same applies to greed or the pursuit of self-interest in economic relations. A greedy person does not have concern for others because all that matters is their own self-interest or the realisation of greedy impulses. As a result, all social relations are superficial. Although witchcraft has been discredited by Western anthropologists as part of an archaic belief system found in primitive societies, the subject of witchcraft remains relevant today from the perspective of comparative studies on greed in modern capitalist societies. In this vein, Robertson writes:

> "Like greed, witchcraft has kept pace with modernity, adapting to the material development of our world, extending the moral index from outrageous consumption to the abominations of accumulation. Greed and witchcraft are critical explanations of behaviour which differ from scholarly theories by incorporating feeling. Because they are locked into our understanding about our lives within the fabric of human relations, they are persistent." (Robertson 2001:104)

Like witchcraft, greed is destructive to human life. Many people's lives have been ruined on an intergenerational basis due to greed. The same has been the case with the effects of witchcraft. Inasmuch as insatiable consumption and endless accumulation of wealth triggers a sense of outrage due to the human lives that are sacrificed in the process, the same sense of moral outrage is felt by those who are inflicted by the scourge of witchcraft. In contemporary Africa, the media is replete with stories where individuals within the employ of government or civil service loot tens of millions in funds that are usually earmarked for welfare purposes, thus leaving thousands of those who rely on welfare programs in a critical state of poverty. Similarly, there are stories where practitioners of witchcraft have destroyed lives of defenceless orphans and widows for reasons that defy any rational explanation. What is apparently clear is that the main commonality between greed and witchcraft is inherent in their destruction to the life of the community or to the wellbeing of the unsuspecting victims.

Sometimes it is difficult to comprehend how someone who is already rich can still defraud helpless pensioners and orphans with the aim of adding more to the millions which he or she already possesses. This type of behaviour defies rationality. Similarly, a witch who kills innocent children for no apparent reason can equally be said to have acted in a way that defies rationality. Witches are believed to not possess any sense of emotion or compassion towards other human beings. In the same way, the effect of greed has remained totally incomprehensible. It appears that capitalism has succeeded in Western societies because of the ability of these societies to embrace greed as an indispensable passion that dominates human nature. The rational explanation that has been given to greed is self-interest. But to what extent can greed promote the common good in a society where greed is morally unacceptable?

An Afrocentric Attempt at Rationalising Greed

Some scholars have argued that African values fundamentally inhibit the appropriation of modern capitalism since they tend to orient towards a distributive approach to wealth. Thus, some developmental theorists have suggested that post-colonial Africa needs to adopt an economic attitude that places emphasis on the profit motive, rather than the prestige motive.

However, Guy Hunter (1967:119) observed that in Africa "the moral element has been equally strong. It is felt as a revulsion against the sufferings and inequalities of growth as it was achieved in the West; a revulsion particularly against private enterprise, not only because it had been disfigured by greed and exploitation but for its association in Africa—capitalism, imperialism, colonialism." The moral element in Africa could not be separated from the political and "purely empirical motives" as demanded by Western capitalism because this moral element had its roots in African traditional culture. He says, "African tribal society and the ethos of the extended family were in many ways egalitarian. Certainly the values of personal thrift and competitive personal enterprise were alien to Africa, in this way Africans were worlds apart from the Puritan fathers of America." What this observation suggests is that America managed to attain world economic dominance because its founding fathers embraced a form of greed that was spiritualised. Conversely, African poverty is rationalised as a manifestation of the absence of greed due to the prevalent moral revulsion against it.

Other scholars have gone as far as to say that capitalism appeared in Africa without the Protestant ethic, which was characterised by an insatiable appetite and endless accumulation of wealth, combined with strict discipline. What facilitated the ascendancy of modern capitalism was the spiritualisation of greed whereby greed was vindicated as being part of the divine plan. As Heilbroner observes, "Acquisitiveness became a recognized virtue, not immediately for one's private enjoyment, but for the greater glory of God" (Heilbroner 1972:33). It is this religious justification of capitalistic acquisitiveness that removed the Western medieval religious sanction against greed. In the context of Africa, some scholars speculate that Christianity and Islam introduced the capitalistic culture of acquisitiveness in Africa from their teaching of individual's personal accountability before God (Van Onselen 1976:186). Others such as Paul

Kennedy argue that the absence of entrepreneurial spirit in Africa was due to African moral traditions. He succinctly points out, "Thus, entrepreneurs who wish to operate within kinship or community situations, where the social pressures against individual acquisitiveness [greed] and mobility are still present and 'big men' are expected to redistribute wealth, must find some way to resolve a central contradiction" (Kennedy 1988:140). Kennedy's observation indicates that African communalism and its prestige motive was an inhibiting factor in the appropriation of Western capitalism, which usually thrives on the assertiveness of individual greed. According to Kennedy, "Church membership provided religious justification, spiritual protection and practical assistance for the converts in their struggle to disentangle themselves from the demands of their wider matrikin and concentrate instead on building up their business and nuclear family interests" (Kennedy 1988:142).

Chapter 5

Greed and the Ascendancy of African Political Capitalism

As previously shown, capitalism was introduced to Africa through the pursuit of individual and collective greed by colonial settlers and their governments, who directly or indirectly supported the colonial enterprises. Colonial capitalism severed accumulation of wealth from hard work and frugality. What we witnessed in colonial capitalism was a situation of racial greed that thrived on subjugation of the natives, coupled with over-accumulation of wealth and luxuries without hard work. There is a general scholarly consensus that Western and American wealth was the result of slavery and the looting and plunder of African natural resources. Colonialism and slavery were also about the siphoning of Africa's natural resources and African labour. Most colonial legislations were aimed at perpetuating Western greed at the expense of systematic deprivation of the majority of black people.

To the present day, assumption of political office is still generally accompanied by the over-accumulation of wealth. In order to have access to wealth, one's connectivity to political power becomes a leeway to unbridled accumulation accompanied by ferocious consumption.

Sometimes post-colonial African greed has failed to benefit the country because the wealth accumulated is often externalised or expatriated to Europe or other external destinations instead of being invested in African communities. Mobuto Sese Seko is on record for having siphoned the wealth of the Democratic Republic of Congo, formerly Zaire, to France, Belgium and Switzerland whilst his country was undergoing national economic decay and excruciating poverty under his leadership. Ascendancy into political office is thus viewed as an opportunity for personal looting of national wealth. It is also on record that in the 1970s, President Siaka Stevens of Sierra Leone "turned the diamond industry into his personal preserve, setting up a private network of Lebanese dealers and local traders to run it for him. By the time he retired in 1985, at the age of eighty, he had amassed a personal fortune estimated at $500 million. Sierra Leone, however, was left decrepit and bankrupt" (Meredith 2005:562). This type of greed is destructive to the common good because it deprives the whole nation of basic livelihoods.

In the case of Nigeria, Meredith observed, "Abacha's greed exceeded that of all his predecessors. It was estimated that he stole more than $4 billion, taking money either directly from the treasury, or from government contracts, or through scams like the Petroleum Trust Fund that he set up ostensibly to channel extra revenue from an increase in the domestic fuel price into infrastructure and other investments" (Meredith 2005:581). It is from such observations that we can glean that ascendancy to political office in post-colonial Africa is mainly propelled by greed—a type of greed that impoverishes a nation. Insofar as greed has been destructive in post-colonial Africa, it has failed to create greater wealth.

In light of the African post-colonial experience, greed emanating from the political sphere becomes lethal to society as a whole. It becomes even more detrimental when there is collusion between state and capital. During colonialism, African leaders were on the same side as their citizens, challenging the colonisers and the unequal economic system. However, in post-colonial Africa there is an emerging partnership between African leaders and the erstwhile colonisers and oppressors. The cultural legacy of colonialism remains through leaders who view the state as a vehicle through which access to the country's resources is guaranteed.

Greed in Africa has become rampant to the extent that leaders can mortgage their countries whilst citizens are unaware of the implications of the deals that they are signing with investors. This is because the issue of accountability has remained elusive in African politics, as the institutions that ought to provide checks and balances on leaders are either weak or do not have the political will to address issues of impunity by leaders and multinational corporations. For this reason, entrance into the political arena of any ruling party has almost always been dovetailed by conspicuous accumulation of wealth at the expense of the poor.

Africa's Response to the Siege of Global Greed

Many scholars have observed that neoliberal capitalistic practices and policies are mainly based on the promotion of the interests of a few at the expense of the majority. The idea of aid and investment maintains that the interests of those who have over-accumulated wealth should have a global reach. The World Bank and International Monetary Fund (IMF) have been wholly committed to the idea that poor African countries can improve their economic situation by sacrificing the poor majority in their midst. For example, the IMF and World Bank prescribed the policy of Economic Structural Adjustment Programme (ESAP) which involved forfeiting the economic wellbeing of the majority in a way that logically benefits the greed of a few individuals; namely, the Bretton Woods Institutions and the multinational corporations that depend on these institutions. ESAP policies achieved this through the legalisation of systematic retrenchments of workers from parastatals that were previously the main employers of the majority of the poor. Clearly, this policy did not promote the needs of the poor.

The idea that the poor will benefit when the greed of a few is left unhindered gained global acceptability through such neoliberal economic policies. Scholars such as Fritjof Capra observed:

> *"Global capitalism has increased poverty and social inequality not only by transforming the relationships between capital and labour, but also through the process of social exclusion, which is a direct consequence of the new economy's network structure. As the flows of capital and information interlink worldwide networks, they exclude from these networks all populations and territories that are of no value or interest to their financial gain... Around the world, a new impoverished segment of humanity has emerged that is sometimes referred to as the Fourth World. It comprises large areas of the globe, including much of sub-Saharan Africa..." (Capra 2002:125–126).*

The implication of this observation is that the globalisation of neoliberal capitalism was aimed at advancing the greed of a few to the exclusion of the majority of the poor. The government is usually advised to not interfere in the free reign of greed because it is presumed to be beneficial to the majority of the poor in the long-run.

However, in post-colonial Africa, governments have introduced economic policies that are aimed at empowering the African elite as a way of taming capitalism. The main presumption is that promoting indigenous African capitalists would eventually lead to the ascendancy of a type of capitalism that has a distinct African flavour. This is intended to counter the expansive nature of Western-led global capitalism that mostly favours North America and its Western allies. The African resentment towards North American and Western-led globalisation arises from the realisation that their greed is depleting African resources. Indigenization policies in post-colonial Africa have thus come from the political front.

Indigenization of Greed

The rationale behind indigenization is based on the idea that colonial capitalism excluded the majority of the Africans from meaningful participation in the national economy. It is argued that under colonialism, the economy was legislatively tailored to benefit whites (who were a minority) while promoting exclusion of the black indigenous African population. It is a truism that colonial capitalism was based entirely on policies of exclusion which ultimately aimed to incapacitate the black person from active participation in the economy.

However, such policies were in accordance with the rationale of greed. At face value, indigenization of capitalist policies aims to domesticate capitalism in a way that allows post-colonial African governments to manufacture African capitalists through legislation. Those who have benefitted from indigenization have become millionaires within a short period of time. The post-apartheid South African government adopted an economic policy called Black Economic Empowerment (BEE), a type of affirmative action, in order to rectify the racial imbalance created during apartheid by giving preference to businesses owned by black South Africans (blacks, coloureds and Indians). The rationale behind this economic policy is that the active participation of blacks as capitalists will result in the wider redistribution of wealth. What has remained unquestioned in such an economic policy is whether greed can ever be capable of creating a situation whereby wealth is redistributed to the benefit of all.

The South African government defines BEE as an "integrated and coherent socio-economic process that directly contributes to the economic transformation of South Africa and brings about significant increases in the numbers of black people that manage, own and control the country's economy, as well as significant decreases in income inequalities" (Black Economic Empowerment Commission 2001:2). The promise inherent in BEE is that of ensuring equality in the economy. The policy is centred on the recognition of decades of inequality under apartheid and seeks to right those economic and political wrongs by supporting black business owners. In this way, the policy is aimed at being a reactionary measure against the greed of the white population.

Obviously, such an economic policy is aimed at active governmental participation in the creation of African capitalists. This policy is often called 'indigenization'. The use of the term indigenization comes from the belief that colonial capitalism was disruptive to the ascendancy of African capitalism in a way that has made Africa too dependent on Western capitalism (Mazrui 1986:164–5; Adedeji 1981:20–36). In this regard, indigenization is partly about the promotion of African greed under the assumption that genuine economic development can only be attained when Africans themselves control their means of production rather than managing a capitalist system that is externally owned. It is also based on the idea that African greed will eventually result in the creation of wealth to the advantage of the majority of the population. In his 'Address to the Botswana University Foundation' the then South African minister of finance, Trevor Manuel, said:

> "... we have come to use the word 'empowerment' in recent years as a broader and more satisfactory characterization of the social policy goal we formerly called 'affirmative action' and before that 'indigenization' or 'Africanization'. Empowerment is partly about redressing historical disadvantage, but it is also about investing in capabilities and opening doors of opportunity. It is a policy objective that infiltrates a very wide range of government and business life—recruitment and training, organizational structure and rules of conduct, procurement, corporate finance..." (Mail & Guardian 2005: 5)

However, as is the case with the rationale of greed, indigenization or Africanization of the economy has always benefitted a few rather than enabling broader economic participation for the majority of the citizens. What has triggered public outcry is that the policies of indigenization have promoted and cushioned the greed of a few individuals who have political connections within the ruling party. In post-colonial Africa, it has become common knowledge that embarking on a political career within the ruling party paves a road to accumulating riches. In Shona culture, there is an adage which says '*Chawawana idya nehama, mutorwa ane hanganwa*'. This literally translates to mean 'when you have a fortune you should spend it with relatives, as one who is not a relative will forget your gesture in the future'. This adage admonishes those in political office to be discriminative towards those who are not related to him when it comes to accessing wealth. Those with relatives who are well-established within the ruling party stand the chance of getting rich quickly without necessarily working very hard. For example, a legislation which requires companies to address empowerment requirements can easily be circumvented by employing the relative of a prominent politician as CEO. The implication here is that a business enterprise will remain in constant need of political protection because political power has become too embroiled in business.

The way indigenization has evolved in post-colonial Africa echoes the sentiments of Thorstein Veblen in *The Theory of the Leisure Class*. For Veblen, those who become capitalists will always act in solidarity on the basis of their long-entrenched, shared economic interests. Thus, he characterised the industrial processes and the economic institutions of the leisure class as follows:

> "*Their office is of a parasitic character, and their interest is to divert what substance they may to their own use, and to retain whatever is under their hand. The conventions of the business world have grown up under the selective surveillance of this principle of predation or parasitism. They are conventions of ownership; derivatives, more or less remote, of the ancient predatory culture.*" (Veblen 1931:203)

In other words, the business world of the leisure class is simply predatory and parasitic in that it feeds on the labour of others, who are denied the luxuries they enjoy. The continued survival of such business practices owes its acknowledgment to past economic outlooks that are based on predation and parasitism. Even in today's society, countries and companies thrive on these characteristics.

The implications of Veblen's theory of Institutional Evolutionary Economics within BEE economic programmes have already been observed by many African developmentalist scholars. Among some of their observations is that BEE economic programmes will inevitably create a class of African capitalists whose economic standing will make it impossible for them to be in solidarity with the majority of the African poor.

Claude Ake advanced the argument that BEE indigenization economic programmes do not necessarily lead to the decolonisation of the African economy as is generally assumed. Such programmes "essentially amount to a new partnership between the African ruling class and international capitalism to their mutual benefit and often reduce areas of conflict between them. By operating under the umbrella of the state, foreign capital reduces the visibility of its exploitation while enjoying new immunities" (1981:39). Ake went on to add:

> "Imperialist exploitation of Africa occurs precisely because of the existence of capitalism in Africa. For the most part, the African ruling class is the creation of Western imperialism and remains largely a tool of Western imperialism. Their interests coincide on the fundamental issue of maintaining capitalist relations of production. The African ruling class survives in so far as capitalist relations of production are maintained, and international capitalism maximizes its exploitation of Africa by keeping African economies capitalist and dependent." (1981:35–36)

Within such an analysis, there is an echo of Veblen's theory that the leisure class (which Ake has identified as the ruling class) tends to form bonds of solidarity based on their own conventional methods of acquiring and consuming wealth. Such solidarity drives the poor to the peripheries of the economy, thus further perpetuating the legacy of economic

imperialism which the BEE indigenization or Africanization policy purports to terminate. It is partly for this reason that other African scholars
have sarcastically argued that indigenization, or BEE, is about the indigenization of privatisation. These scholars refute the traditional argument
that has often been proffered by advocates of indigenization, which says
that indigenization of capitalism avoids the externalisation of profits that
are made on African soil. Related to this is also the claim that international capitalism thrives on the mobility of capital—that is, foreign
capitalists can easily relocate their business operations to other countries
or regions depending on the profitability of such a venture.

Countering these arguments, Chanda Chisala asserts that we should
accept capitalist practices as they are practised all over the world and concentrate on improving our African economic environment. He writes:

> "The only way is to change our environment and this will start
> by changing our attitude to the whole idea of capitalism. Capi-
> talism simply means allowing the environment to be as free as
> possible. We destroy the environment when we start intervening
> in it in order to force our ideas of who should own what, how
> much he bought what for; how should this one pay that one; who
> should pay less taxes than who; etc... The answer to our economy
> simply lies in a true understanding of the capitalist philosophy,
> period. And the logic is really simple: the most capitalist nations
> in the world are the richest countries in the world—can it get
> simpler than that? It really has nothing to do with constitutions
> (even though we do need a good constitution); with foreigners;
> with foreigners; with agriculture; or even with national airlines."
> (Chisala C. "Indigenization of Privatization [Part 2]: Some Gen-
> eral Comments on Privatization and Capitalism", Accessed 22
> April 2007)

Chisala's argument is that African states should embrace capitalism as it
has been practised in the Western world. Programmes that tend to go
against the logic of the capitalist system can only be counterproductive.

This capitalist logic is based on the idea that in economic matters, the free market should decide who gets what and who deserves what. A whole-hearted embrace of capitalism would also entail that states do not enforce legislations that aim to aid a particular segment of the population against the other.

It has been observed by many scholars that in order to benefit from BEE or economic policies of indigenization, one has to be well-connected politically, by being a relative or a friend of a prominent politician. Those who are well-connected are always offered business opportunities in the form of tenders. Through these tenders, a small group of Africans have been able to become millionaires within a short period of time. Although the idea of correcting the imbalances created by apartheid is noble, the manner in which this is being carried out has resulted in little difference being made to the general population who suffered under it. In fact, it has been observed that BEE has been manipulated by political and economic elites. BEE compliance has become imperative for any tenders that are submitted to government to the extent that politicians and high-level technocrats often collude with those in business regarding how these tender documents are to be submitted.

Tenders have been legislated in a way that promotes greed amongst those who are politically well-connected. The legislation of tenders has been called 'Affirmative Action' whereby the government purposefully offers business opportunities to black people due to their legislative exclusion under apartheid. It is therefore an act of justice to accord black people with economic benefits that they were previously denied. However, ironically, the process of economically empowering black people has tended to benefit only a minority of Africans. The rational explanation for this lies in the working of greed in human economic relations. The issuing of tenders has been characterised by a system of briberies, kickbacks and a spectrum of underhand dealings. In a way, it can be said that the policy of BEE or indigenization has inhibited blacks from becoming 'genuine' capitalists in the traditional Weberian sense of accumulating wealth through hard work, thrift and frugality. These policies have promoted a certain type of greed that does not necessarily promote the ascendancy of natural capitalists, but capitalists who are entirely enticed by the pursuit of parasitism. These empowered African capitalists do not necessarily have to work hard for their wealth; rather, the road to endless accumulation of wealth rests in their political connectivity.

For this reason, African political capitalism has often been regarded as 'crony capitalism' that is usually divorced from entrepreneurship as understood in the traditional modus operandi of modern capitalism. These newly empowered African capitalists have been aptly referred to as 'tenderprenuers' in the sense that the source of their wealth is mainly derived from government tenders. When these 'tenderprenuers' are entrenched in government tenders as the source of their wealth, they seldom embark on any other meaningful business initiatives besides monitoring, initiating, crafting and managing tenders. Through government tenders, the politically well-connected have been able to become millionaires often in the space of a year. Thus, tenders have been seen by many critics as the unleashing of assisted greed from which only a few have benefitted.

On the surface, BEE was purported to equally share out the economic cake among those who were formerly disadvantaged; ironically, those who were previously excluded have continued to exclude each other from the national economic cake. Political capitalism should thus be seen as a reaction against the colonial exclusion of the Africans from meaningful participation in the economy. For example, in the embryonic stages of colonialism, Africans were mainly seen as labourers. Felix Gross said in reference to the most notorious colonial capitalist and empire builder, Cecil John Rhodes, that in order to make Africans work for him, Rhodes had to devise a plan. "It called for special enticement to lure them to the farms, and a good psychological understanding of their primitive though complicated mentality to keep them there. Cecil found out that many Natives needed money to pay their hut-tax. He lent them the money on their promise to work for him. And they never let him down. 'Kaffirs', he wrote home, are really safer than the Bank of England" (Gross 1956:11).

Political capitalism is partly based on the realisation that African labour was abused under colonialism. Hendricks Verwoed, who was the Minister of Bantu Affairs at the time, stated, "There is no place for the Bantu in the European Community above the level of certain forms of labour. It is of no avail for him to receive a training which drew him away from his own community and misled him by showing him the green pastures of the Europeans but still did not allow him to graze there" (See Lipton 1986:24). In such utterances, it is abundantly clear that colonialism or apartheid was mainly motivated by greed. Metaphors such as 'green pastures of the Europeans' and 'did not allow him to graze there' imply that colonialism or apartheid were very much closely related to acts of beastly economic behaviour, whereby political power was used to promote the greed of white people to the exclusion of the blacks.

In post-colonial Africa, there was an ardent belief that political control should be complemented by economic control. "While missionaries implored the colonial subject to lay up his treasures in Heaven... the traders and administrators acquired his minerals and land. There was no intention of processing locally the discovered raw materials. These were intended to feed the metropolitan mills and plants to be exported back to the colonies later in the form of finished commodities" (Nkrumah 1970:22). According to Nkrumah, colonialism was a political epoch that was mainly concerned with the expropriation of African resources. He adds:

> "In her African colonies, Britain controlled the export of raw materials by preventing their direct shipment to foreign markets. After satisfying the demands of her home industries, she sold the surplus to other nations and netted the profits herself. The colonial farmer and worker had no share in those profits. Nor was any part of them used in providing public works and social services in the colonies." (Nkrumah 1970:22–23)

In light of such utterances, one can say that some African nationalists viewed colonialism as a mechanism for promoting the greed of colonial masters as well as systematically looting the resources of the colonised. Thus, the advent of political independence was followed by what Julius Nyerere called 'economic nationalism'.

According to Nyerere, "economic nationalism was about deliberate control of national resources." He avers:

> "Such an economic expression of nationalism is nothing new in the world; although the manner of the action may have been peculiarly Tanzanian, its motivation is common enough. Every country—whether it be capitalist, communist, socialist or fascist—wants to control its own economy... At independence we achieved political control, but all-important industries remained in foreign hands...Whatever economic system the peoples of different African countries eventually adopt, it is quite certain that sooner or later they will demand that the key positions of their economy are in the hands of their own citizens." (Nyerere 1968:262)

It is evident that the post-colonial concept of economic nationalism was concerned with the post-colonial quest to control capitalism nationally instead of leaving this economic system in foreign hands. For this reason, an externally controlled capitalism was deemed exploitative.

In his pursuit of economic nationalism, Nyerere became very hostile to the whole concept of economic growth and development through direct foreign investment. He writes:

> "... I do not think there is any free state in Africa where there is sufficient local capital, or a sufficient number of local entrepreneurs, for locally based capitalism to dominate the economy. Private investment in Africa means overwhelming foreign private investment. A capitalistic economy means a foreign dominated economy. These are the facts of Africa's situation. The only way in

which national control of the economy can be achieved is through
the economic institutions of socialism." (Nyerere 1968:264)

Nyerere saw capitalism in Africa as an economic system that was externally controlled by virtue of its early connection to colonialism. As someone who held moral sentiments, he wholly believed that socialism was the answer to the realisation of economic nationalism. Socialism was a moral economic system because it enabled equity among citizens by providing equal opportunities to gain wealth. Here it can also be inferred that Nyerere's preference of socialism over capitalism was based on his distaste towards the greed that went hand in hand with capitalism.

However, those who argue against the idea that colonialism was based on the expropriation of African resources maintain that since African traditional values were prohibitive to the appropriation of capitalism, there was no way in which Africa could have adopted capitalism without colonial intervention. In other words, Africa would have remained poor and backward if association with Western economies did not occur. In this vein, one of the most notorious and dogmatic defenders of the providential nature of colonialism, A. J. Hanna, did not mince his words:

> *"... It is virtually certain that conditions in Africa would still be roughly what they were a century ago, had it not been for the introduction of European administration, European instruction, and contact with the European economy. It has often been asserted that investment in Africa involved injustice to the Africans, since it was a device for draining the wealth of their continent into the pockets of investors in Europe. This is an elementary misconception. The mineral and other resources of Africa were useless to the native inhabitants until they were developed, and they could not be developed without transport, machinery and skill. By making these things available the European investor, however self-interested he may have been, was serving Africa; and if his enterprise came to an end through bankruptcy, Africa gained nothing through his misfortune." (Hanna 1961:11–17)*

Hanna's main argument is that colonialism was morally justifiable on the grounds that it allowed the African economy to accrue economic benefits from its contact with the Western world, which would have been otherwise impossible. Hence, Hanna suggests that colonialism was in favour of the Africans. The expropriation of African resources was justifiable because those resources were not being used at all.

In previous discussions on colonial capitalism, we have encountered arguments by scholars who state that Western imperialism destroyed traditional economies without necessarily substituting them with an authentic capitalist foundation as a substitute (Mazrui 1986:215). However, some African scholars have gone as far as to claim that the Western world was the real force behind capitalism in post-colonial Africa. On the basis of this, it is argued that the second phase of Africa's struggle for independence is to be focused on economic decolonisation because the present post-colonial African economy is a remnant of colonialism or apartheid. In the same vein, Chinweizu states, "Political decolonization and formal independence in Africa have not meant a change in the guise of imperialism. Political decolonization has not been accompanied by economic decolonization" (Chinweizu 1999:769).

The idea of economic decolonisation has fuelled the post-colonial African economic policy of BEE indigenization or Africanization. The post-colonial African economic orientation has been mainly about wresting control of their economies from their prior oppressors—the West. Chinweizu goes on to say:

> "On economic decolonization, the African states and the West were in sharp conflict. The African states wanted to wrest control of their economies from a West which was determined to retain that control. For the West, losing control would mean giving up what a century of conquest and colonization had achieved for them, and what political decolonization had aimed to preserve. For the African states, however, not to wrest away that control

would be to defeat the economic aim of their struggle for political
independence." (Chinweizu 1999:771)

Hence, economic decolonisation was mainly about curtailing the greed
of the West. Phrases employed by Chinweizu such as 'wrest control' and
'losing control' highlight the animalistic nature and force by which this
was done. Chinweizu went on to say that the Africanization of capitalism could not succeed because the Africans who were supposed to
be the agents of this policy "had enormous appetites for material consumption". As a result, "they craved the best that the industrial world
could offer, and were therefore preoccupied with the distribution for
consumption of whatever income was available from an economy which
remained colonial in character."

However, contrary to the economic behaviour of African capitalists,
"the bourgeoisie of the Western core were habitual accumulators of capital, highly experienced at it, and with highly developed productive or-
ganization as well as vast sums of already accumulated capital which they
could deploy for further accumulation" (Chinweizu 1999:790). In other
words, creating a group of African capitalists who are responsible for the
domestication of capitalism will not succeed because the consumption
habits of African capitalists are in opposition to the spirit of accumulation found amongst Western capitalists. A similar argument is posed by
Nkrumah:

> *"Thrift has not been a characteristic of our people, largely be-*
> *cause they have not enjoyed enough income to make the ques-*
> *tion anything but academic. How to instill a need to spend and*
> *save wisely among them has become a major preoccupation now*
> *that they are beginning to enjoy higher incomes and the taste for*
> *amenities. Our family system actually discourages family heads*
> *from saving, for the system, in effect, penalizes the man with ini-*
> *tiative in favour of the lazy and the weak. The indigent members*
> *of the family live upon the more fortunate ones… At the present*
> *time, the man who makes a reasonable living finds his money*

> *eaten up by his relatives… so that he simply cannot meet his personal obligations, let alone save anything." (Nkrumah 1970:100)*

The above quote implies that post-colonial African economic behaviour was mainly inclined towards ostentation, where wealth is seen as something to be shared with relatives rather than saving for further accumulation in the future. Thus, African traditional customs that encouraged sharing posed a stumbling block to the ascendancy of capitalism in post-colonial Africa.

The other implication is that the ascendancy of capitalism is only possible when people are selfish instead of being generous to their fellow human beings. When individuals accumulate wealth and refuse to share it with others, they create an economic situation whereby wealth is over-accumulated and concentrated in the hands of a few individuals. These individuals, as we have seen previously, may be greedy but end up becoming benefactors to society at large. It is this neoliberal capitalist thinking that allows policies such as BEE or Africanization to benefit a few Africans while sidelining the vast majority. Ultimately, these few beneficiaries fuel a situation whereby indigenized African capitalists emulate the accumulation and consumption habits of other capitalists all over the world.

Political Capitalism and Emulation

Some post-colonial African critics have argued that it is futile for the African government to enforce polices aimed at creating a class of African capitalists. Some scholars such as Claude Ake claim that those who benefit from governmental economic intervention in favour of BEE align themselves with the practices of international capitalists and are not in solidarity with their fellow African poor (Ake 1981:32). This idea finds its logic in Thorstein Veblen's theory of Institutional Evolutionary Economics in which the practice of economic predation is a shared characteristic amongst capitalists despite their backgrounds because "in order to stand well in the eyes of the community, it is necessary to come up to a certain, somewhat indefinite, conventional standard of wealth…" (Veblen 1931:30). According to Veblen, this predatory habit has no explanation besides the seeking of power and prestige through endless accumulation and acquisition of wealth. The appetite for this among capitalists is insatiable. The drive to acquire more wealth becomes addictive to the extent that it becomes compulsive.

The main reason behind this is that those who have accumulated large amounts of wealth desire to emulate those of the same class as themselves, thus setting a path to an endless psychological state of competitive accumulation without stipulating standards of sufficiency. Within this state, the individual severs himself or herself from communal belongingness. As Veblen puts it, "The quasi-peaceable gentlemen of leisure, then, not only consumes of the stuff of life beyond the minimum required for subsistence and physical efficiency, but his consumption also undergoes a specialization as regards the quality of the goods consumed. He consumes freely and of the best, in food, drink, narcotics, shelter, services, ornaments…" (Veblen 1931:73). According to Veblen, such consumption habits are a way of expressing one's economic solidarity with other members of the leisure class.

However, such conspicuous consumption habits are to be maintained by the individual in order to remain honourable within the circle to which they now belong. For example, those who have become millionaires as a result of BEE tend to socialise with other beneficiaries of BEE. Amongst themselves they discuss their business interests and future plans, and they are commonly known to compete in hosting the most expensive parties amongst themselves. It is primarily for this reason that developmental economists such as Ake maintain that BEE or indigenization does not necessarily lead to the decolonisation of the economy. For Ake, such policies "amount to a new partnership between the African ruling class and international capitalism to their mutual benefit and often reduce areas of conflict between them. By operating under the umbrella of the state, foreign capital reduces the visibility of its exploitation while enjoying new immunities" (Ake 1981:39). In other words, foreign capital is cushioned when it enters into partnership with the beneficiaries of BEE/Africanization.

The partnership between the beneficiaries of BEE and international capital perpetuates the continuous drainage of African resources to the detriment of the majority the African citizens who derive no benefit. This collaboration amounts to the continuation of imperial exploitation as it was during the times of colonial capitalism. Ake emphasises this point:

> "Imperialist exploitation of Africa occurs precisely because of the existence of capitalism in Africa. For the most part, the African ruling class is the creation of Western imperialism and remains largely a tool of Western imperialism... their interests coincide on the fundamental issue of maintaining capitalist relations of production. The African ruling class survives insofar as capitalist relations of production are maintained. And international capitalism maximizes its exploitation of Africa by keeping African economies capitalist and dependent." (Ake 1981:35–36)

Ake's analysis echoes Veblen's theory in that the leisure class (which Ake has identified as the 'ruling class') tend to form bonds of solidarity based on their own conventional methods of acquiring and consuming wealth. Such solidarity drives the poor to the peripheries of the economy, further perpetuating the legacy of colonial capitalism. It is partly for this reason that other African scholars have sarcastically argued that in reality, BEE indigenization is the indigenization of privatisation.

Economic policies of BEE indigenization have hindered the externalisation of profits that are made from African soil. Those who have profited from BEE indigenization often externalise their profits to the Western world instead of investing in Africa, where the profits are accrued. In this way, BEE beneficiaries actually impoverish their African countries. The Western world has imposed punitive measures against most African beneficiaries on the grounds that they have been found to have properties and bank accounts in the West. Beneficiaries are also widely known to send their children to study in Western universities rather than national African universities. Despite having derived their wealth from African policies, their behaviour and actions do not reflect a sense of concern for the wellbeing of their native countries.

Although BEE indigenization was aimed at promoting economic nationalism, the reality is that it has ended up promoting the spirit of greed among its beneficiaries. Polo Hadebe conceded that it was difficult, in light of the present codes, to regulate those who are using BEE for their own personal enrichment: "But how do you determine how rich is rich enough… Even if we were ready to go the route of regulation, would these guys give us access to their balance sheets? Much of their wealth is still on paper too. We would start entering murky territory" (*Mail & Guardian*, April 20–25). The problem with such an economic policy is that it is crafted in a way that inevitably leads to the enrichment of a few at the expense of the majority.

The argument is that BEE policies have created a situation whereby beneficiaries of these policies have continued to accumulate wealth. For example, Vuyo Jack has noted that after accumulating lots of wealth through BEE deals, Mzi Khumalo "notified the public that he was no longer available for BEE deals." Jack goes on to observe:

> "Herein lies a good lesson. Once BEE beneficiaries operate in the mainstream economy without the need for assistance envisaged by BEE, they should no longer monopolize the opportunities presented by BEE but allow other people to use the policy to gain access to the mainstream economy. The principle of graduation is simple—if one graduates, the school will soon become too full and all students will suffer… The graduation from BEE will most commonly be based on wealth levels, which government cannot set. Individuals must determine their own graduation level." (Jack & Haris 2007:59–60)

To describe a situation in which one individual becomes a multimillionaire within a short period of time and voluntarily resigns from the system as 'a good lesson' is to trivialise the impact BEE has had on the actual performance of its beneficiaries as genuine capitalists. Here I argue against Jack by saying that graduation in essence is marked by a completion of a certain set of requirements that are known and accepted by everyone. As stated above, Jack's understanding of BEE graduation is based on the idea of self-determination that is mainly informed by self-satisfaction through accumulation of wealth. However, he cites only one graduate as an adequate representation of the whole BEE empire of accumulation—this cannot be considered a representative sample!

The most difficult issue to understand with regards to the rationale behind BEE is the qualifications which one must possess in order to become a beneficiary. This has to be understood in the light of political capitalism in post-colonial Africa, whereby the BEE Africanization policy empowers the same individuals who in most cases are well-connected to national centres of political power. As Jack states:

> "The more influential the politician, the greater the attraction
> the suitors have for him or her. Furthermore, the more deals
> the former politician can conclude, the more bankable he or she
> becomes as a deal-maker and the stakes get higher. The trend is
> evident when tracking the deals entered into, for example, by To-
> kyo Sexwale, Cyril Ramaphosa and Saki Macozoma. Their early
> transactions were smaller in value but increased substantially
> as they landed more deals. BEE does not intentionally advocate
> empowering the same individuals. Companies seeking Black own-
> ership credentials frequently choose the same individuals and
> do not cast their nets wider in search of other Black people to
> partner with." (Jack & Harris 2007:60)

As previously mentioned, BEE Africanization does not empower the majority of the African population that was previously disadvantaged by colonialism and apartheid. This policy was designed to promote the greed of a few who are politically well-connected at the expense of the majority. The only plausible explanation as to why the same individuals would continue to access more BEE deals can only be linked to their political connectivity. In other words, the proximity of BEE beneficiaries to the political sphere makes them suitable candidates to be chosen by companies as partners. Being close to politicians who are in close proximity to political power means also to benefit from government tenders, as BEE beneficiaries often use those well-connected politicians as their 'front-men'. On final analysis, BEE or Africanization is not aimed at empowering the majority of black people who have been previously dispossessed by apartheid or colonialism. It is simply a misguided policy, prompted mainly by political opportunism and the insatiable desire of African politicians for a luxurious life without any concern for the well-being of multitudes of the poor who were previously disadvantaged. To what extent can we say beneficiaries of BEE do have a concern for the wellbeing of the majority of the poor? What capability can such a policy have towards equitable economic development?

A persistent complaint that has been levelled against BEE is not only that such an economic policy promotes greed among indigenous Africans, but also that it encourages a culture of looting with impunity. A common practice of BEE indigenization beneficiaries is to acquire shares in order to sell those shares at a higher price. This type of business behaviour has been described by other beneficiaries of BEE as 'casino' mentality. Anthea Jeffery highlights the prevalence of this in post-colonial Africa: "Businessman Mzi Khumalo provides a classic example of this alleged 'casino' mentality. In 2001 Khumalo persuaded the state-funded Industrial Development Corporation to lend him the money he needed to buy 10.7 million shares in gold-mining company Harmony Gold at a significant discount" (Jeffery 2014:155–156).

From literature on BEE and indigenization, it remains unclear whether BEE beneficiaries are business people in the Weberian sense. What has remained indisputable, however, is that beneficiaries of BEE

Africanization have used their proximity to political power for self-serving purposes in a way that does not promote the common good. Jeffery goes on to say that "… instead of remaining a BEE partner and using his shareholding to increase black control over the corporation, as the BEE script envisaged, he quickly persuaded his colleagues in Harmony's BEE consortium to sell their shares to him. In 2003, a scant two years after the deal was concluded, he proceeded to sell all the shares at his disposal at a profit of R1 billion. This boost to Khumalo's personal wealth came at great cost to Harmony…" (Jeffery 2014:156). Beneficiaries of BEE are not only inflicting harm to the economy or companies they loot from, but their quest for personal accumulation of wealth negatively affects the wellbeing of the majority of the African poor.

The main critique of BEE is that the policy has continued to benefit the same individuals. Jeffery states, "Many ordinary South Africans said the principal effect of BEE ownership requirements had been to give more and more wealth to the 'usual suspects' within the ANC, many of whom were already millionaires and sometimes even billionaires" (Jeffery 2014:156). We can deduce from the above quotation that political capitalism in post-colonial Africa has not been egalitarian; rather, it is poised at promoting the greed of a few who are politically well-connected. In this regard, entrance into politics is synonymous with entrance into wealth. It can be said that politics is not about working *for* the common good but has instead become a gateway to over-accumulating wealth *at the expense of* the common good.

The government of Zimbabwe went as far as to introduce a ministry of indigenization in which it was gazetted that "at least *fifty-one per cent* of the shares of every public company and any other business shall be owned by indigenous Zimbabweans" (*Gazette* 2008, March 2008, Part II). However, those who are able to own 51% only includes those who are already rich and not ordinary poor Zimbabweans. There is overwhelming evidence that wherever indigenization has been implemented in post-colonial African states, it has always benefitted a select few who have access to political power. Companies have recruited these politically influential Africans on their company boards with the aim of gaining protection from policies that might compromise their business interests. Those who get access to national wealth often abuse such opportunities. Sometimes those who are awarded tenders have performed jobs to an exceptionally low standard, to the extent that governments have ended up losing millions of dollars, thus contributing directly to national under-development. Yet because of their political connectivity these individuals cannot be held accountable or asked to repay the money they have wasted. For example, African newspapers are replete with stories of individuals that are given contracts to undertake particular projects which they either do not deliver or deliver to an inferior standard. This practice is obviously detrimental to the economy.

BEE/Indigenization as Part of the Grand Narrative of Mistaken Policies

There is strong evidence that BEE indigenization or Africanization has never developed the post-colonial African economy. Some scholars such as Adebayo Adedeji have observed that indigenization as a development policy has evolved through various stages. He writes:

> "As a policy, however, one gets the impression that the approach to its development and application has been rather ad hoc, piece-meal and lacking in internal consistency. It has been a product of circumstances, and at times mainly of politicians reacting to unfavourable economic situations and the demands of small groups of indigenous businessmen who felt that the prevailing economic conditions put them in an unfair position vis-à-vis their foreign competitors. It was hardly the original work of development planners, although their involvement became inevitable after political decisions have been made. Just as the articulation of a policy of indigenization came about in a piece-meal fashion, so the measure for its realization was equally ad hoc and unplanned." (Adedeji 1981:45)

The above observation implies that BEE or indigenization does not reflect a well-considered or well-planned economic policy aimed at fostering national economic development. Instead, the creation of this policy aimed to create competitive African capitalists who would contend with other foreign capitalists in terms of consumption and wealth accumulation. In this regard, BEE does not provide any developmental merits that are beneficial to national development. If this is the case, the question that naturally arises is: why implement such a policy?

The problem with this policy from an economic development perspective is that it is tailored to promote the greed of a few while excluding the majority who were previously economically marginalised under colonialism. Some scholars have attempted to rationalise the policy in terms of African political reaction to multinational capitalism. In line with this, it is maintained that indigenization enables African participation in multinational capitalism. Ali Mazrui asserts:

> "The economic interests of the newly westernized Africans become interlinked with those of the multinationals at some levels. More and more jobs within the multinationals become accessible to the locals. More and more decision-making roles are Africanized. Increasingly the faces behind the managerial desks are local. Increasingly the boards of directors co-opt westernized locals to lend further legitimacy to their operations." (Mazrui 1978:294)

The crux of Mazrui's observation is that the economic interests of indigenized Africans cannot be separated from the interests of multinational companies. In fact, these companies use the indigenized Africans to further their own economic interests. For this reason, we can say that the aim of indigenization was partly to give a local semblance to multinational capitalism by co-opting local personnel.

As for the indigenized Africans, colluding with multinational capitalist allows them to pursue their economic interests. Mazrui goes on to say that "the growth of the market for Western consumer goods partly depended on the spread of Western tastes and lifestyles. Some aspects

123

of African culture have reinforced the temptation to emulate and imitate the West. Most of Western political and economic culture has been conditioned by the respect given to both political individualism and the profit motive" (Mazrui 1978:295). It is the indigenized Africans who are instrumental in the dissemination of Western tastes and appetite for luxury among the westernized Africans. The accumulation of wealth by the indigenized Africans does not necessarily benefit the African economy; rather, as stated previously, this wealth is externalised, to the detriment of the post-colonial African economy. While proponents of BEE indigenization have always maintained that the policy is aimed at transferring colonial capitalistic institutions into African hands in order to regain effective control, African dependency developmental theorists still argue that such a policy can only lead to solidarity between African capitalists and global capitalism.

Critics of African political capitalism (BEE/indigenization) maintain that the economic power of foreign-owned companies has managed to successfully contain the momentum of expropriation of their wealth through post-colonial political capitalism. It is partly on these grounds that African dependency theorists often maintain that African capitalists are contributors of post-colonial African underdevelopment. By way of illustrating this point, Chinweizu adduced that:

> "Nigeria's inability to accumulate and properly invest its enormous oil income was largely due to the origins, ideology and aspirations of its governing class. The dominant section of the elite were mandarins, largely originating from the non-producer sections of the colonial petite-bourgeoisie... On the other hand, they had enormous appetite for material consumption. Forgetting that hunting is not the carcass on the plate, they conceived development planning as the making of shopping lists of modern artifacts to be imported and consumed. They craved the best that the industrial world could offer, and were therefore preoccupied with the distribution for consumption of whatever income was

124

*available from an economy which remained colonial in charac-
ter." (Chinweizu 1999:789–790)*

Thus, the tragedy of political capitalism in post-colonial Africa is that
it created a culture of consumption; a type of capitalism that did not
promote local investment, but the drainage of wealth in a way that was
advantageous to international capitalism. Whilst Nigeria has been one
of the leading oil producers in the world, it has remained an exporter
of crude oil since the times of colonialism. The export of crude oil has
always benefitted those who are politically well-connected within the
ruling elite, through collaboration with multinational companies. It is
for this reason that BEE is not seen as an appropriate developmental
policy in post-colonial Africa; it promotes the indigenization of greed as
opposed to economic development.

Another problem is that the beneficiaries of this policy are not business people by calling. By receiving lucrative tenders from the government, beneficiaries can—and have—become multi-millionaires in under five years. As mentioned previously, some people have facetiously
coined beneficiaries of BEE 'tenderpreneurs' since the main source of
their wealth is through the receipt of government tenders, rather than
personal entrepreneurial initiative.

However, one of the most abominable practices prevalent within the
system of tenders is that a person who has no experience and knowledge
within a field can be awarded a tender of enormous value. For example,
someone with very little experience in civil engineering can be awarded a
tender worth millions of dollars to construct roads and bridges. Usually,
the beneficiary of such a tender will subcontract real engineers for $100
million whilst he or she pockets $50 million for doing virtually nothing.
Some politicians have been vocal against this practice. For example, the
current South African minister of higher education, Blade Nzimande,
was vehement in his condemnation:

> *"Tenderpreneurs, found in both public and private sectors, and often the two colluding, are those who corruptly capture government tenders using their political positions or connections. In fact, 'tenderpreneurs' pose the single biggest threat to genuine entrepreneurs, as the latter often do not have inside information or the necessary political connections to get government or even tenders in the private sector. 'Tenderpreneurship' expresses the intersection between holding of political position and business interests." (Nzimande 2010:2)*

The practice of tenders has been characterised by underhand dealings that are protected by politicians from public scrutiny. Samson Zondi observed that "the practice of tenders has become synonymous with kickbacks and underhand dealings such that a perception has been created that South African is a corrupt state. It is however important to note that instead of creating entrepreneurs, South Africa has witnessed the mushrooming of 'tenderpreneurs' who rely on criminal underhand deals to secure tenders" (Zondi 2012:45). However, this practice of underhand dealings in the practice of tenders is something unique to post-apartheid South Africa, and in many post-colonial African countries it has been the main avenue for wealth acquisition. An opportunity to hold political office has become synonymous with the opportunity to accumulate endless wealth for oneself and one's relatives and friends. Two years ago, Kenyan people carried pigs to the newly elected parliament in protest against the dominant political culture of greed and looting. Whilst Africa as a continent is beset by the problem of poverty, African politicians have continue to pass legislations that legalise an uncontrolled looting of wealth, excluding the majority of the African population living in abject poverty. Thus, political capitalism in post-colonial Africa has perpetuated poverty in a manner far worse than that which existed under colonial capitalism.

Politics in post-colonial Africa has inhibited the rise of genuine entrepreneurs on the basis that there should be reparations for the previously disadvantaged black people. Moeletsi Mbeki states that whilst South Africa has all the necessary properties for a modern liberal capitalist society.

> "The one missing factor is support for entrepreneurship from both the politically dominant black elite and the dominant economic elite, who are protected from domestic and foreign competition by the political elite in return for reparations. The consequences of the disappearance of entrepreneurship is part of the ideology that South Africa's political and economic elites are becoming manifest with every passing day." (Mbeki 2009:95)

Whilst liberal capitalism is based on the idea that there should not be interference in the running of the economy, political capitalism has given rise to a situation whereby the national economy has been cornered by political and economic elites. This collusion inhibits the ascendancy of a spirit of entrepreneurship in post-colonial Africa. Here the problem is that political office is being used to promote the looting of national resources by individuals who are not capitalists by calling. Although there is no empirical evidence to suggest that the implementation of BEE has promoted economic development, many African politicians have continued to endorse such policies for self-serving purposes rather than for the benefit of national economic development.

Moeletsi Mbeki took an extreme position on this matter by referring to African politicians and the empowered African elites as 'architects of poverty'. He said the central theme of his book was based on "the way the powerful in Africa instead of enriching their societies sell off the continent's assets to enrich the rest of the world. In return for this service these powerful Africans—who I call the political elites—receive the crumbs from the tables of the foreigners who make their fortunes by processing Africa's resources" (Mbeki 2009:xi). It is an empirical fact that Africa as a continent is endowed with plentiful natural resources. However, these resources are usually sold as raw materials to foreign companies overseas who process them and sell them back to Africa at exorbitant prices. It is a truism that newly empowered African business people have not endeavoured to begin the process of processing raw materials into finished products. Their main focus is in exporting raw materials to overseas companies—a business venture that benefits overseas companies while impoverishing African economies. In much of Africa, goods are exported as raw materials without much effort towards downstream processing and value addition. This exposes Africa to unfair trade practices. A most telling example is that of cocoa farmers in West Africa, who still struggle with low pay, rudimentary technologies and unfair labour practices; meanwhile, chocolate manufacturers make millions of dollars in profit every year. Several reports have highlighted the disparity between cocoa farmers in Africa and chocolate manufacturers.

However, beneficiation and value addition of Africa's natural resources is expected to develop African economies and to ensure that African citizens get fair prices for their products. So pertinent is the idea of beneficiation and value addition that the continental body and regional economic communities (RECs) have embraced this message in the quest for a peaceful and prosperous Africa. In fact, in 2014 the Southern African Development Community (SADC) Summit's theme was 'SADC Strategy for Economic Transformation: Leveraging the Region's Diverse Resources for Sustainable Economic and Social Development through Beneficiation and Value Addition'.

The idea that Africans should have control of their natural resources and be able to process these natural resources by themselves is a noble but unrealistic one, until and unless instituting policies ensure that raw resources are extracted and processed into locally manufactured finished products before being exported to overseas markets. The post-colonial African failure to utilise its raw materials into finished products is seen as the main reason for the continuation of poverty. Such a situation creates a vicious circle of dependency whereby the African continent remains in total dependency, both financially and technologically. For example, most African scientific departments or research centres do not introduce scientifically innovative ideas, but are more concerned with interpreting scientific discoveries from other parts of the world. The lack of funding for scientific research has created a situation whereby external funders (who are usually from North America and Western Europe) monopolise what should be disseminated as scientific knowledge in the African context. In most cases, such knowledge has to serve the economic interests of these external funders. Ali Abdel Gadir states, "The substantial contributions foreign donors are making to social sciences research [in Africa] has given the donor community substantial power which has brought with it a number of intended and unintended constraints on social science research" (Gadir 1994:109). In other words, external donors control the production and dissemination of knowledge in Africa. Within such a scenario, it is obvious that that which is produced and disseminated as authentic knowledge caters to the interest of the donor rather than the recipient. An African academic who promotes West European and North American economic and political interests in Africa is more likely to receive donor funds for his or her research compared to those whose writings are considered to be radically Afrocentric.

Moreover, due to the legacy of colonialism, African universities and other tertiary institutions have been designed to serve Western and North American interests. Mazrui observed that, "African universities became nurseries for Western organisational skills. African universities became nurseries for a Westernised black intellectual aristocracy. Graduates of Ibadan, Dakar and Makerere acquired Western social tastes more readily than Western organisational skills. Those graduates became steeped in Western consumption patterns rather than Western productive techniques" (Mazrui 1994:119). This has had a debilitating effect on Africa's socio-economic development because even those in educational institutions, who have the opportunity to open up a discourse surrounding the issue of corruption, are instead dedicated to promoting ideas which serve the West rather than their own countries.

Political Capitalism and the Misappropriation of Capitalism

Political capitalism has often been considered the main reason for the misappropriation of capitalism in post-colonial Africa by scholars. Hernando De Soto (2000:4) argued that the failure of capitalism in non-Western countries cannot be attributed to culture alone. He claims, "The disparity of wealth between the West and the rest of the world is far too big to be explained by culture alone. Many people want the fruits of capital, so much that many are flocking to Western nations." De Soto goes on to suggest that non-Western societies do not benefit from capitalism due to their failure to emulate the West in how they produce capital. While non-Western countries "already possess assets, they need to make a success of capitalism, they hold these resources in defective forms: houses built on land whose ownership rights are not adequately recorded, unincorporated businesses with undefined liability, industries located where financiers and investors cannot see them." Here, De Soto makes a critical point. In post-colonial Africa, people own houses and parcels of lands without title deeds. This is partly due to the legacy of co-lonialism in which legislation decreed that Africans could not privately own land. Most Africans were forced to settle in communal land owned by a chief or a king on behalf of the community. Hence, political cap-italism in post-colonial Africa has not reversed the colonial legacy, but has kept it intact.

To the present day, many Africans still do not possess title deeds to their properties and the land they own. Without title deeds, most Afri-cans remain without property and lack surety to access loans and other lines of credit. Thus, the majority of wealth in rural areas remains dead capital because it cannot be registered at the national stock exchange. Occasionally, when a mineral has been discovered on land that is owned by a particular family, the government can easily lay claim to that land and demand the family to relocate in order to begin mining operations.

The affected family cannot resist or resort to courts for redress due to the absence of title deeds to the land in question.

Another argument that is closely related to the misappropriation of capitalism in post-colonial Africa is related to the theory of evolution. For example, De Soto attributes the failure of capitalism in non-Western societies to evolution. He observes, "Americans and Europeans have been telling the other countries of the world, 'You have to be more like us'. In fact, they are very much like the United States of a century ago, when it, too, was a Third World country" (De Soto 2000:6). From this we can infer that the poverty that is rife in post-colonial Africa and other Third World countries can be explained rationally in terms of evolution—in other words, that those who are poor are merely on the lower rungs of the evolutionary ladder. Inherent within this idea is also the presumption that post-colonial Africa and other Third World countries will evolve and eventually become like the industrialised West and the USA.

In the same vein, Moeletsi Mbeki propounded, "Capitalism in the West has moved a long way from the days of mercantile capitalism; it went through the stage of industrialisation and Western countries are now referred to as post-industrial societies. The problem with Africa is that it is still locked in the mercantile stage of capitalism. The challenge facing the continent is how to modernize capitalism from mercantilism to industrialism" (Mbeki 2009:xi–xii). It can be inferred from this statement that not only should Africa industrialise in a fashion similar to the West, but that the earth is endowed with enough resources to enable all countries to become as rich as Western countries. Here, the salient assumption is that the resources of the earth are inexhaustible. Critics of post-colonial political capitalism such as Mbeki confidently presume that there is an abundance of resources that can enable African states to become as rich as the West. This is linked to a notion embedded in neoliberal capitalism. According to this notion, the economy has to keep on growing for the sake of the greater good. However, what is not taken into account in this line of thinking is that one cannot keep on growing without experiencing old age! Natural resources are depleting and some of them are not renewable.

Without colonial intervention, Africa would have evolved into a different economic system that differs remarkably from the Western capitalistic economic system. The prevailing idea that post-colonial African society should develop in a way similar to the USA and the West is extremely unrealistic since the economies of the latter were built on systematic plunder and looting of human and natural resources from non-Western countries. For example, the economic prowess of America has been built on slave labour, of which the issue of reparation has remained contentious. Similarly, the British economy has been built on decades of plundering resources from the colonies of its former empire. Precious minerals, artefacts and timber from colonies were considered possessions of the Crown, to be plundered at will for the construction of the British economy. While Britain does not have a single gold mine in her territory, today it possesses the largest gold reserve in the world—a factor that has made the British pound the strongest currency in the world. When former colonies request financial assistance from Britain or America, they are usually told that their economic and political policies are the main reason behind their poverty and perennial economic underdevelopment. Most poor African countries that request financial aid from Britain usually do so in pursuit of reparation rather than charity or humanitarianism.

As mentioned previously, in contemporary times, wars have been fought in order to gain access to a particular resource from a militarily weaker country. For example, a strong scholarly school of thought maintains that the war in Kuwait in 1990 was not necessarily undertaken purely on humanitarian grounds, but was motivated by the need to procure cheap oil by USA and her Western allies. The adviser to President Bush is on record for saying, "Even a dolt understands the principle. We need the oil. It's nice to talk about standing up for freedom, but Kuwait and Saudi Arabia are not exactly democracies. If Kuwait's export was oranges, there would be no issue" (Vaux 1992:9). The West's need for access to cheap oil has had catastrophic consequences; this can be seen in the current destabilisation of the Arab world. The rationale behind going to war in order to access cheap oil makes sense when one takes into account the fact that most of the 'developed' world relies heavily on air transport for most of its travel purposes. In the case of the Democratic Republic of Congo, the country has been subjected to perennial civil war due to its vast natural resources. When a country is in a state of perpetual civil war its borders become porous; a situation that enables foreigners to plunder its resources without any payment. The plundering of resources in the DRC is the root cause of the endless civil war. The modern war is being fought on the basis of the need to control the resources from foreign lands by force. As a way of encountering the hegemony of Western capitalism, African political capitalism has adopted an ethnic approach to capitalism.

Greed, Political Capitalism and Ethnicity

In post-colonial Africa, there is an emphasis on giving political capitalism a degree of local cultural semblance. As indicated previously, African traditional communities have been mobilised to form business associations or co-operatives. For example, Contralesa (Congress of Traditional Leaders of South Africa) "decided to move the politics of ethnicity into the marketplace. Having established a business trust a year earlier in order to join a mining consortium, they were about to create a for-profit corporation to pursue investment opportunities in minerals, forestry, and tourism; formal application had been made to register the company" (Comaroff 2009:7). Thus, the relationship between ethnicity and economic development remains pivotal to the domestication of capitalism in post-colonial Africa. The rationale is that colonial capitalism deprived African communities of their traditional economic livelihoods.

Yet the question as to whether local communities have a right to the resources naturally found in their areas of residence has remained a controversial one. John and Jean Comaroff observed that current neoliberal capitalistic practices have commodified cultural traditions. "If they have nothing distinctive to alienate, many rural black South Africans have come to believe, they face collective extinction. Identity from this vantage, resides in recognition from significant others, but the kind of recognition, specially, expressed in consumer desire" (Comaroff 2009:10). Thus, what has made ethnicity economically lucrative and marketable is the inherent desire of different ethnic groupings to be recognised as culturally distinct. This is evidently a sale of culture which is "replacing the sale of labour in the Brave Neo-South Africa…" (Comaroff 2009:11). Advertisements have capitalised on ethnicity more than ever before.

> "But the process may also, often does, open up a politics of dissent, especially when investment capital from the outside plays into inequalities within local populations: in its most brute form, when ethnic elites, by one or another means, exploit new opportunities and compatriots. This may not undermine ethnic identification among the latter; to enrich themselves to the disadvantage of their less well-positioned kin, neighbors, and contrary, it may undermine its importance as an object of both possibility and political struggle." (Comaroff 2009:12–13)

The trading in of ethnic identity benefits a few—especially those who impose themselves as custodians of cultural traditions, such as chiefs and kings—at the expense of the majority of fellow citizens who belong to the same ethnic group. Since political capitalism thrives on patronage, a few individuals are usually given the privilege to use ethnic identity in their business ventures on the basis of their ability to deliver desirable political outcomes to the ruling party. Ethnic identity features are not necessarily owned by a single individual; rather, one finds that they are owned by all members of the community by virtue of their common belonging. Trading in identity has become central to political capitalism in post-colonial Africa. It is therefore not uncommon to find companies that are named after African indigenous terms. The Comaroffs stated:

"The identity industry is a prime case in point. Those who seek to brand their otherness, to profit from what makes them different, find themselves having to do so in the universally recognizable terms in which difference is represented, merchandised, rendered negotiable by means of the abstract instruments of the market. Ethno-commerce feeds an ever more ubiquitous mode of production and reproduction, one born of a time in which, as we have noted, the sale of culture has replaced the sale of labor in many places." (Comaroff and Comaroff 2009:24)

The idea of naming companies under indigenous names has become commonplace in post-colonial Africa. This can be interpreted in two ways. The first interpretation is supported by the Comaroffs when they maintain that such a practice is a way of trading in identity, or wanting to have one's ethnic identity visible in the capitalistic market place. The other, more credible interpretation is that these indigenous names are primarily aimed at authenticating the domestication of capitalism in post-colonial Africa. Under colonial capitalism, it was abundantly clear that the type of capitalism being implemented intended to subjugate the majority of the African population and their resources in the hands of the colonising powers. In Southern Africa, companies such as Anglo-American gold mining company, De Beers, Lever Brothers and Lon-Rho (London Rhodesia), to name a few, undoubtedly imparted the message that the economy was under foreign control. Accompanying this foreign control was the domination of the economy by foreign owned companies as well as rampant expropriation of Africa's natural resources.

The idea of trading in identities is partly based on the quest for being recognised culturally as well as globally. However, trading in ethnic identities is not necessarily a new phenomenon. It is a common practice, found in many countries all over the world. For example, German, Chinese and Japanese companies have names that clearly exhibit their ethnic origins. This practice has been described by many scholars, such as John and Jean Comaroff (2009), as the capitalistic commodification of culture or a trade in cultural identities.

In colonial Africa, as the Comaroffs observed, ethnic objects "were extracted as raw material, refashioned, and transacted by Western elites 'entirely free' of native control" (Comaroff and Comaroff 2009:29). The authors go on to claim that "having substituted universal citizenship for ethnic identities at home—in theory at least—these worldly regimes appointed themselves custodians of 'tribal' peoples overseas, peoples whose lifeways, aesthetics, and material possessions were deemed all of a piece with their lowly status on the evolutionary scale of human types" (Comaroff and Comaroff 2009:29–30). In this way, the colonial condition thrived on the manipulation of the identities of the colonised for self-serving purposes. For example, during colonialism, Native Reserves or homelands were divided along ethnic lines although they were not suitable for human habitation.

Within post-colonial Africa, the trading in of ethnic identities has been championed by the African elites, who in most cases are the main beneficiaries of economic indigenization policies. Currently, we are witnessing a surge of BEE front companies that use indigenous tribal names for their own personal companies. For example, in South Africa, many companies are using the traditional concept of *ubuntu* to name their companies. Although these BEE companies frequently use communal cultural identities, usually the community at large does not benefit from them. These companies use the local communities for the sole purpose of expropriating the natural resources and their identities for personal economic gain. It is not unusual for newly discovered resources to be exploited not for the benefit of the whole national populace, but for the benefit of a few individuals who use tribal or ethnic identities to benefit from tenders and exploit the newly found resources. A thorny issue related to the use of ethnic identities while trading and conducting business is that some of the individuals who receive government tenders have no professional expertise in the services they purport to provide. Here one can justifiably conclude that corruption and political capitalism are inextricable from one another.

Chapter 6

A Symbiotic Relationship between Corruption and Greed

What is the root cause of Africa's socio-economic problems? If you pose this question to most African citizens, the common reply is 'corruption'. This widespread belief corroborates with evidence that has been produced by various researchers, including those from Transparency International and the Afrobarometer Survey. According to Transparency International (2015), corruption has had devastating consequences in Africa, mainly by perpetuating poverty in the continent. A more recent report by Transparency International (2018) indicates that Africa still ranks first in terms of levels of perceived corruption.

Additionally, the Transparency International report highlights the trust deficit that exists between citizens and government, by noting that the majority of African citizens feel that corruption is on the rise and that there is nothing they can do about it. Corruption in Africa comes in many forms, including individual level corruption and abuse of public office for political gain. Thus, corruption can range from micro-level actions such as bribes offered to civil servants in exchange for public services, to much more serious acts such as embezzlement of funds and abuse of state resources.

Corruption in Africa has become endemic; it not only erodes the moral fabric of society but undermines democracy and hinders development. In fact, reports have shown how countries in Africa lose billions of dollars every year because of corruption. This corruption comes in many forms. One such form is illicit financial flows from the continent, which have become a matter of major concern due to their negative impact on Africa's development and governance agenda. This can be seen in the emergence of tax havens that have helped multinational companies to hide their immense profits overseas, and as a result, avoid tax. In fact, in 2015 former South African president Thabo Mbeki presented a report on the illicit financial flows in Africa which estimated that around 50 billion dollars is siphoned annually from Africa by multinational corporations. The UN Economic Commission for Africa (UNECA) presented a similar report in 2017, highlighting that this figure had doubled to 100 billion dollars.

However, the issue of corruption is complex and requires a multi-faceted approach to understand. There are many sources of and reasons for corruption, which need to be understood holistically. They can be categorised into the following: historical, socio-economic, political, institutional and individual. Among these causes are issues such as ethnicity, tribalism, nepotism, patronage and the appropriation of power for economic rent—just to mention a few. However, scant attention has been given to the relationship between corruption and greed. Many scholars have often discussed corruption in a way that suggests greed and corruption are entirely unrelated.

Corruption is regarded as the primary cause of post-colonial Africa's economic and political problems. From a developmentalist perspective, many scholars have traced Africa's economic underdevelopment to corruption since those in political office tend to hoard national resources solely for personal gain. A telling example is that of Kenya, which has been rated one of the most corrupt countries in Africa. Although Kenya's anti-corruption laws and strategies have been in place since 1956, the country remains dented by corruption at all levels. Successive Kenyan governments have seemingly been unable to deal with the malaise of corruption, despite the existence of enabling legal and policy framework (The Ethics and Anti-Corruption Commission) and public pronouncements by political leaders against corruption. So endemic is corruption in Kenya, that it affects not only public offices but also other actors such as the opposition. A story showing how public officials aided the importation of tainted sugar into the tainted markets made headlines in July 2018. This was followed a month later by news of how corruption in public offices and collusion with the private sector led to illegal constructions on riparian land, including state of the art shopping malls, offices and apartments. This resulted in a directive from the National Environmental Management Agency (NEMA) to destroy all buildings that were unlawfully built on riparian land. Although efforts to correct the environmental wrongs were laudable, billions of Kenyan shillings (millions of United States dollars) inevitably lost value as a result of the demolition of buildings that were on riparian land. Clearly, this type of corruption results in loss of livelihoods for citizens as well as a weak national economy.

The potential to accumulate riches is seen as the main advantage of being in public office. In many parts of Africa, there have been instances in which politicians have emptied public coffers for personal use as they are concerned with their own interests, rather than the common good. Despite becoming multimillionaires after looting public coffers, public officials often continue doing so. This shows that they have lost sense of what is sufficient; in this sense, their actions cannot be given any rational explanation or justification. As we have seen in the preceding discussion, greed makes individuals act in ways that defy any form of rational explanation. For a greedy person, there is no satiability when it comes to accumulating wealth.

In this regard, we can say that corruption is a manifestation of individual greed within the public sphere. For this reason, most of the policies that are promulgated by African politicians are usually aimed at legalising corruption. Most post-colonial rules that have been enforced through an Act of Parliament usually benefit those in politics and public servants, who are responsible for the practical enforcement of these acts. It is in this process that the situation resembles a situation of hyenas in a feeding frenzy over a carcass. For example, one of the channels through which corruption becomes rampant is through the implementation of tenders and procurement, where the practice of kickbacks and nepotism has become the norm. Corruption is at the heart of the narrative of greed in post-colonial Africa, and it is a practice that has contributed immensely to Africa's underdevelopment.

Corruption, Greed and Africa's Economic Underdevelopment

While there are numerous factors at play—including the unequal global geo-political environment, the unfair trade terms and the legacy of colonialism—it is undeniable that corruption ranks highly as one of the main factors behind the underdevelopment of Africa today. Corruption impedes economic growth by discouraging foreign and domestic investment; taxing and dampening entrepreneurship; lowering the quality of public infrastructure; decreasing tax revenues; diverting public talent into rent-seeking and distorting the composition of public expenditure.

Some scholars have argued that corruption in Africa is the main culprit behind Africa's economic underdevelopment, since most economic opportunities are given to relatives or friends of those who hold political power. Corruption in post-colonial Africa has marginalised the majority into the periphery of the economy and is dominated by a few who are politically connected. John Mbaku observed:

> "In Africa, most people see corruption in more practical terms:
> the theft of national resources; embezzlement of funds from public

*accounts; illegal taxation by public servants with the benefits ac-
cruing to them and their relatives and friends; nepotism and the
granting of patronage; extortion of bribes in the distribution of
public goods and services... prostitution of one's public office in
an effort to generate extra-legal income; capricious and selective
enforcement of state laws and statutes in an effort to generate
benefits for the office holder; and differential treatment of private business enterprises in the expectation of an illegal payment
from the business owner whose enterprise is granted favorable
treatment." (Mbaku 2000:12)*

Similar to greed, corruption implies a lack concern for the wellbeing
of others and the common good. The standard definition of corruption
used by many scholars is "the abuse of public office for private gain"
(Beets 2007:70). This definition is very similar to the standard definition
of greed, which means to act in a way that deprives others of the same
goods which one enjoys. As we have seen previously, the word 'greed' has
been replaced by the word 'self-interest' by economists. *The Shorter Oxford English Dictionary* (1973:1934) defines self-interest as being solely
concerned with "one's personal profit, benefit, or advantage" as well as
"regard to, or pursuit of, one's own advantage or welfare, to the exclusion of regard for others". In the economic teachings of the Church Fathers, the term 'self-interest' was equated with terms such as usurpation,
covetousness and interest in one's economic well-being whilst excluding
those of others (See Troeltsch 1931:116; Shewring 1948:6–12; Gonzalez
1990:216–219). Usage of the term became prevalent during the Age of
Enlightenment as a substitute for the ecclesiastical term 'greed'.

The transition from greed to self-interest was introduced by economists in two forms. Albert Hirschman observed that two elements have
been developed by economists to describe a character that is driven by
self-interest. The first observation is that self-interested individuals give
predominant attention to the consequences of contemplated action for
themselves. In this regard, they act only after calculating the potential

benefits to be accrued from undertaking a particular decision or action. Secondly, relations of self-interested individuals will always reflect a systematic attempt at evaluating costs and benefits to themselves when a particular action has been done (Hirschman 1977:9–30; cf. Smith 1976:56; Wicksteed 1946:166). Such behaviour is a demonstration of greed, in that one acts without any degree of concern for others and solely in pursuit of that which is advantageous for the individual. A greedy person rarely takes into account the impact of his or her actions on others, especially those who are not closely related.

However, if greed is deeply embedded in the workings of liberal capitalism, to what extent can this economic system be severed from corruption? As shown previously in the writings of classical Western scholars such as Bernard de Mandeville, human vices that are commonly condemned are in actual fact a vehicle for society's progress and growth. Philip Wicksteed echoed Mandeville's sentiments when he stated that capitalistic economic relations have nothing to do with morality, and that asking moral questions about economic relations is purely misdirected. In this regard, he says, "The economic forces and relations have no inherent tendency to redress social wrongs or ally themselves with any ideal system of distributive justice" (Wicksteed 1946:169–170). In other words, within the liberal capitalistic economic system, every form of behaviour is acceptable.

The idea that there is a symbiotic relationship between corruption and greed is well articulated by Mbaku, "Whereas corruption in the post-independence period has allowed a few individuals to amass enormous wealth for themselves, it has generally impoverished and marginalized the African peoples and prevented the government from devising and implementing effective poverty alleviation programs" (Mbaku 2000:17). When a few individuals amass wealth for themselves at the expense of the majority, the only plausible explanation is that such individuals are driven by greed. Sometimes this wealth accumulation results in the whole economy becoming a preserve of the families of corrupt government individuals. In post-independence economic situations which were predominantly capitalistic, this economic system (which was inherited from colonialism) had all the conditions conducive to the flourishing of corruption in post-colonial Africa. For example, by virtue of the advent of capitalism through colonialism, white people throughout the colonial era felt entitled to hoard material possessions without any sense of concern for the ethical imperative towards public accountability. As we have seen previously, colonial capitalism was characterised by legalised looting in which corruption, when practised by white people, was not considered as such. Instead, it was given anthropological and political respectability and considered a mere manifestation of apartheid.

Corruption and Post-Colonial Economic Transformation

The resentment of the African population towards capitalism (which ultimately led to its failure) stems not only from the political consequences of colonialism but the corruption that has become associated with this economic system. The support for socialism in post-colonial Africa, which was reminiscent of the African traditional ethic of collectivism, was partly based on a sense of moral indignation towards the prevalence of corruption in independent Africa. This was observed by Mazrui, who says, "[A] factor which predisposes many Africans in favour of socialism is the rampant corruption among the immediate post-colonial rulers of the continent" (Mazrui 1989:284).

Moreover, socialism was found to be more appealing because of its ethical similarities with African traditional collectivist values, in which sharing of material possessions is highly esteemed as an expression of one's humanness or *ubuntu*. In traditional African societies, an individual with a moral disposition (which manifests itself as living harmoniously with others in the community) is regarded as a real human being compared to one who puts ultimate value on material acquisitions. In traditional societies, a morally sensitised person does not place utmost value on 'material wealth'. Rather, he or she believes in equality, so that no one can be envious of another and no one can control others by virtue of their position, whether in society or in an organisation (Gelfand 1981:15–16). In the Shona language, the word *huori* (corruption) literally translates to mean 'rottenness'. A corrupt person has no concern for the wellbeing of others. Such a person is thus deemed to be devoid of any humanness; someone who uses people for selfish ends without a sense of concern for the other person's wellbeing. It is for this reason that someone who is endowed with huori has no sense of concern for the common good.

There have been two competing schools of thought with regards to corruption in Africa. The first school of thought maintains that corruption is viewed as antithetic to African cultural traditionalism, which placed concern for the community above individual lust for wealth. This has been identified as the 'prestige motive' and is central to traditional African cultural attitudes towards wealth, whereby it is seen as being there for communal enjoyment. The prestige motive was explained by Benezet Bujo when he observed that sharing wealth with others was a highly commendable cultural practice, such that a person who failed to do so could not hope to prosper in his or her business endeavours. According to Bujo, "Business enterprise [for a selfish person] will not flourish, property will be lost, or the family of the owners will be struck by sickness, that is, the neighbour with whom one is unwilling to share may turn into a sorcerer" (Bujo 1998:162). It can be said that in traditional African societies, corruption was countered by the prestige motive. The other school of thought maintains that the prestige motive can provide a rational explanation for corruption in post-colonial African society.

The Prestige Motive and Corruption in Africa

It is indisputable that the ethical values most highly esteemed by African culture place emphasis on the primacy of harmonious relationships with others in the community. The desire to help others and to be considered a good and generous person is the summation of what it means to be a *munhu chaiye* (someone who is sensitive to the needs of others) who has *ubuntu/hunhu/botho*. Someone endowed with humanness finds actualisation in caring for the material wellbeing of others, and sharing material goods with others serves the communal 'identitarian' function of an individual's common belongingness. Individual belongingness is usually expressed in the form of sharing with the community. In the following quote, Bujo reflects on the prestige motive:

> "...the border between avarice and frugality is unclear in Africa because saving money, for instance, could be taken as an excuse for refusing to offer necessary assistance on others. This may explain why even today people in Africa do not hesitate to organize big feasts with relatives, friends and acquaintances and to spend money lavishly in order to keep human contacts as close as possible." (Bujo 1998:163)

The problem that arises in this type of behaviour is that the urge to please relatives can easily give rise to a situation whereby the individual ends up partaking in corruption. In African culture, relatives sometimes comprise of a whole village and one is expected to support them by giving gifts and sometimes providing employment opportunities for them. In this way, the prestige motive can also result in nepotism in order to appease relatives. One can conclude that when the prestige motive is facilitated by corruption, the end result is a situation where tribal greed becomes predominant, promoting the needs of those who belong to one's tribe and immediate community at the exclusion of others.

The prestige motive has strongly affected African politics in that political office is now regarded as a way to easily access the national purse. The promotion of the prestige motive through political and corrupt activities can easily degenerate into huori or corruption in the whole public sector. Over the course of time, such dishonest practices become extremely difficult to extinguish from the functioning of governmental institutions.

Robert Jackson echoes this idea when he says, "While corruption occurs whenever officials accept bribes, corrupt governments can develop only where such practices are widespread and are sustained by social attitudes…" (Jackson and Rosberg 1984:278).

In post-colonial Africa, the traditional social and cultural attitudes which encourage individuals to share their economic fortunes with relatives, instead provides the acceptance of corruption as integral to the promotion of the prestige motive. One frequently finds that the prestige motive is extended by the ruler to his subordinates as a way of rewarding their loyalty. Positions in the public sector are usually given to relatives of the president even when they lack the relevant qualifications. Sometimes, for example, a minister prioritises the provision of electricity to a village of the president's relatives, thus ensuring that the gesture will be returned in kind by the president in the near future.

Here, Jackson and Rosberg did not overemphasise when they said that if rulers condone corrupt activities, then the society they lead is bound to condone corruption as a way of life. Corruption is unlikely to occur in a social context where the ruler submits all government machinery to constant checks against corruption. "But if the ruler or other prominent leaders indulge in such [corrupt] practices themselves, then the demonstration effect upon the rest of the country can be profound because such practices can reinforce existing social expectations in which family, friends, associates, clients, clansmen, and tribesmen have higher claim on a public official's conduct than do government rules and regulations" (Ibid). It can be said that the prestige motive urges rulers and public servants to do everything in their power to meet the expectations of their relatives and friends, rather than professional conduct and the formal expectations of their jobs as civil servants.

When corruption is entrenched in the upper echelons of power, failure to partake in corrupt activities can easily endanger one's political career. Corruption and the prestige motive that goes with it has become the trademark for the monopoly of political power in post-colonial African politics. Once political power is monopolised, there is often a blatant disregard for the ethos of public accountability. Instead, this becomes 'relativised' for politicians and public officials to only include loyalty to one's family, friends, clients and tribesmen and the party. It is mainly within these circles that the prestige motive is expressed through looting of government coffers and national resources. It is not uncommon for national resources to frequently be used to promote the prestige motive as a means of entrenching permanent political grip on power; for example, by showering the electorate with gifts and ostentatious banquets. As well as the prestige motive, some scholars have argued that African culture has some general characteristics that make it fertile ground for corruption to thrive.

The Relationship between African Culture and Corruption

Culture plays a critical role in the way we relate and respond to the realities that surround us in the world. To have a fuller understanding of another human being requires us to know the cultural background they were raised in. Cultural phenomena must be relativised if we are to make sense of the diversity that characterises our human existence. Culture helps people to enter into a dialogue and make sense of that which has been externally introduced into a particular society. When Christianity was first introduced in Africa as a foreign religion of the 'oppressor', African culture served a prophylactic role in the process of perception and interpretation of its message and the meaning behind that message. The subject of interpretation and deciphering the meaning of phenomena that present itself in human existence is known as hermeneutics, a term translated from Greek into English meaning 'interpretation'. Since human existence consists of plurality in being and doing, the same applies to our interpretation of phenomenon and the understanding that arises thereafter. In a world that is dominated by a consciousness of multiculturalism, the ideal—or what one might say is the illusion of homogeneity in human modes of being and understanding—has been surpassed with the reality of cultural epistemic pluralism.

Fabien Eboussi Boulaga observed that in this world of multiculturalism, dialogue takes precedence over monologue. He states:

> *"When the humanity of various groups is thus formed by investiture in particular content, issuing from their 'dialogue' with a singular nature and a singular temporality, they immediately assign absolute priority to what differentiates them from one another. The foreigner will be a mere semblance and caricature of a human being. Convergence, similarities of content are sought only where none can be the victor, where one is forced to admit and accept the humanity of the other, in whole or in part." (Boulaga 1984:165)*

Put simply, multiculturalism is sometimes characterised by the tendency to want to dominate the other by presenting one's own cultural perspective as the absolute reality which everybody is expected to follow.

Corruption is not an ethical problem that is exclusively found in African societies and other underdeveloped societies. Corruption exists even in so-called developed societies, but it is concealed or disguised in formal legal enactments. In this vein, Douglas Beets expounds:

> *"In poor countries, for example, grand corruption is often considered flagrant, and petty corruption viewed as widespread. Many consequently consider these nations to be corrupt while wealthier, developed countries are perceived as relatively free of corruption. Corruption in developed nations, however, may exist in the accepted, legal forms of political contributions and extensive lobbying expenditures which may yield, for individuals and businesses, immunity from certain laws, monetary resources from tax relief, government subsidies..." (Beets 2007:71)*

In other words, in developed countries corruption is practised under the guise of the widely accepted instrument of the law. The law is so deeply embedded in cultural practice that anything promulgated as a law is accepted as part and parcel of cultural social organisation. The developed world, especially the West, has often accused non-Western countries of being corrupt on the salient presumption that in the African context, the commission of corruption is without any legal concealment or justification. Theodore H. von Laue advanced the idea that this is simply the result of the world's attempt to imitate the West. He writes, "We have westernized the world also in the images of our minds, in the structures of our thoughts, essentially unchallenged. No other people has been able to impose its way of looking at the world on so many others outside its culture" (von Laue 1987:376).

What is not taken into account is the reality of cultural diversity in the interpretation and understanding of corruption. This results in a monolithic definition of culture, or a Eurocentric definition of corruption. For example, the most widespread definition of corruption which has been used by many scholars is derived from a non-governmental organisation called Transparency International. Transparency International define corruption as "the misuse of entrusted power for private gain" (See Beets 2007:71). It is evidently clear in this definition that corruption means undertaking one's public duties or responsibilities for the advantage of oneself. This definition is problematic when corruption is committed for the benefit of the community, as is the case in the traditional African prestige motive. In the context of Africa, corruption often occurs due to the fulfilment of traditional communal cultural responsibilities. Among the Shona people of Zimbabwe there is a popular adage which states, '*Chawawana idya nehama mutorwa ane hanganwa*' meaning 'What you have found should be shared with relatives because a stranger can easily forget'. In such proverbs, the greed that is channelled to promote the wellbeing of one's blood relations is justifiable on the grounds that it guarantees some reciprocity in the form of material favours in the future. Put crudely, it can be said that it becomes a type of investment for the future.

This links to the idea of 'group selfishness' as propounded in social biology, which shows that a group with greedy members who are only concerned with the interests of their tribe are more likely to be the most successful in life's competition for existence. For example, a tribe that becomes economically stronger than other tribes is more likely to dominate tribes that are poorer. Some scholars have postulated that many wars in post-colonial Africa have been fought along tribal lines whereby the economically strongest tribe has always triumphed and ruled over weaker tribes. The term 'tribe' can be used interchangeably with the word 'ethnicity'. A tribe or an ethnic group, as Masipula Sithole observed:

> *"Has traits or unique attributes such as language (dialects therefrom), religion, custom, etiquette, dress and the like which distinguish it from others. These traits are often taken for granted until the group encounters another group possessing different traits. Group awareness occurs when a group recognizes its differences from other groups. But, mere difference and an awareness of it is of no consequence, it is the emotive or subjective interpretation of the differences that is of consequence."* (Sithole 1985:184)

The existence of traits in other tribes that differ from one's own raises the problem of tribalism.

Another Shona proverb admonishes, '*Ukama igasva hunozadziswa nokudya*' ('Relationship is a half measure that finds fulfilment in eating with others'). This proverb is an exhortation to a person who belongs to the same tribe that he or she should share his or her wealth with relatives. This sharing of wealth is an expression of one's relatedness in actuality. Within the group, the spirit of tribalism remains salient and is only aroused when there is competition for scarce resources (Sithole 1985:184–185). However, the above proverb is contradicted by another proverb which says, '*Usahwira honukunda ukama*' ('Bonds of friendship can be stronger than blood relations'). It is in such sayings that one is reminded that life is characterised by contradictions to the extent that it is folly for one to rely entirely on blood relations, as is the case with staunch tribalists.

However, belief in tribalism and its causal influence on corruption relies heavily on upholding one's identity among other tribes. A Zulu proverb states, '*Izandla ziyagezana*' ('Hands wash each other'). This implies that one must always reciprocate in kind whenever a gift or favour has been given. It can also connote that one should always remember their indebtedness to others and repay their debts whenever an opportunity to do so presents itself. In African culture, reciprocity is a highly valued custom. It suggests one's ability to recognise the existence of others by doing that which is beneficial for them. When someone has been good to you, African culture requires that one should show gratitude by returning the favour. In Shona language, the above Zulu proverb finds its equivalent in the following proverb, '*Kandiro kanoenda kunobva kamwe*' ('A small dish of food goes whence another small one comes'). In the English language, this proverb finds its equivalent in one which says, 'One good turn deserves another'. Sooner or later, people are expected to reciprocate a gift they have received. This proverb can be quoted to refer to a person who, in his days of prosperity, turns a deaf ear to the needs of his neighbour, but in his time of need goes to the neighbour for a favour (Hamutyinei and Plangger 1987:53).

The logic behind such proverbial wisdom leaves the door open for kickbacks in the awarding of tenders through BEE policy. As a result, BEE has become entrenched in a vicious cycle: the practice of kickbacks is usually reciprocated by more kickbacks, which results in an economic situation where the beneficiaries of BEE have remained the same. The dominance of kickbacks has created an association of BEE beneficiaries, similar to an elitist cult, and has made it difficult to introduce an all-inclusive approach that enables economic access to the majority of the population.

BEE economic policy can be well-understood when subjected to Thorstein Veblen's theory of the leisure class. Through certain cultural

153

practices of gift giving, beneficiaries of BEE have formed families of an affluent class, whose habits of accumulation can only be described as predatory. The accumulation of wealth remains unexplainable as it is gained through kickbacks and bribery. This is expounded upon by Veblen as follows: "But as fast as a person makes new acquisitions, and becomes accustomed to the resulting new standard of wealth, the new standard forthwith ceases to afford appreciably greater satisfaction than the earlier standard did" (Veblen 1931:31).

In post-colonial Africa, the few who have benefited from BEE have remained its permanent beneficiaries. It is an ongoing reason for continuous agitation among post-colonial African scholars, on the grounds that upon closer scrutiny, BEE is based on the pursuit of individuals' self-seeking behaviour while excluding the majority of their fellow citizens. What creates a culture of economic exclusivity in BEE is the obligation to reciprocate a previously received favour. In this instance, the practice of reciprocity is not necessarily a virtue.

Other anthropologists have argued that it is a social practice that is based on self-interest. For example, Marcel Mauss in his study of Scandinavian culture (where the practice of gift-giving was prevalent) deduced that in such cultures, the idea of gift-giving was just "a polite fiction, formalism, and social deceit" because the driving motive was "economic self-interest" (Mauss 1990:3). Thus, the practice of gift-giving was another way in which primitive societies pursued their economic self-interests. However, what Mauss is saying does not contain anything of novelty. As we have seen previously, other pioneers of liberal capitalism in the West such as Bernard de Mandeville poeticised greed by suggesting that all of our human economic relations are fundamentally motivated by it. Mandeville would agree that gift-giving is not a genuine expression of generosity, but fictionalised greed. What this claim implies in actuality is that the receiver of a gift is expected to return it back in a way that gratifies the original giver.

However, gift-giving is not unique to African culture and other non-Western cultures; it is a common practice even in the West. Aafke Komter researched the social practice of gift-giving in the Netherlands and deduced that it serves various functions that have nothing to do with the giver expecting to be paid back in future by the receiver. He states that gift-giving "symbolizes the unique, highly valued, personal, and durable character of relationships. These gifts are not intended to evoke return gifts and seem mainly to be given out of sympathy, love, or the need to support another person." In this cultural context, there is no expectation from the giver that the gift should be reciprocated in kind. Komter went on to observe that, "Within families, money is sometimes given by (grand) parents to their grown-up children, just to offer some monetary relief or to make up for some more structural shortage of money. These gifts are unidirectional: no returns are expected, and even when the gift is given in the form of a loan, the expectation of return is vague and not specified in time" (Komter 2005:26–27).

Despite this, if gift-giving is 'unidirectional', the implication here is that the giver is self-sufficient in every respect—that is, materially and emotionally. Although the giver of the gift may not expect material repayment of the gift, is it not possible that the giver may expect some remuneration in the form of emotional gratitude? Gratitude is usually expected from all cultures whenever a gift is given; the giver of the gift expects to be thanked by the recipients. In doing so, the recipient of the gift is in fact reciprocating, and the gift does not necessarily require to be met with a material gift in return. Therefore, there is a need to move away from the notion that a beneficiary must express appreciation to the giver, be it materially or financially. There are other non-material means of expressing gratitude and maintaining positive social relations which need to be embedded in the way we interact with others.

Corruption and the Gift of Life in the Biblical Tradition

According to the book of Genesis, God used the deluge to blot out all life created on the earth because of the evil deeds of humanity.

> *"Now the earth was corrupt, in God's sight, and the earth was filled with violence. And God saw the earth, and behold, it was corrupt; for all flesh had corrupted their way upon the earth. And God said to Noah, 'I have determined to make an end of all flesh; for the earth is filled with violence through them, behold, I will destroy them with the earth. Make yourself an ark of gopher wood..." (Genesis 6:11–13)*

Noah is said to have been spared from the deluge due to his righteousness, and it was on the basis of his righteousness that all forms of life on earth were to survive God's wrath through the flood. When God spared Noah his life, Noah reciprocated the gift of life by giving God a gift in the form of a sacrifice.

> *"Then Noah built an altar to the Lord, and took of every clean animal and every clean bird, and offered burnt offerings on the altar. And when the Lord smelled the pleasing aroma, the Lord said in his heart, 'I will never again curse the ground because of man, for the imagination of man's heart is evil from his youth; neither will I ever again destroy every living creature as I have done'." (Genesis 8:20–21)*

As an expression of his gratefulness towards God for sparing his life and that of his household, Noah offered God a sacrificial gift, the delicious smell of which is said to have led God into repentance for having destroyed life on earth. However, God is said to have reciprocated Noah's sacrifice with a gift in the form of a blessing to him and his sons.

In the Jewish religion, as shown in the prophetic tradition, God or Yahweh did not take delight in Israel's gifts in the form of temple sacrifices. Rather, what Yahweh delighted in was a gift in the form of righteousness in peoples' hearts. In the book of Amos, Yahweh is said to have rebuked the Israelites' gifts as follows:

> *"I hate, I despise your feasts, and I take no delight in your solemn assemblies. Even though you offer me your burnt offerings and cereal offerings, I will not accept them, and the peace offerings of your fatted beasts I will not look upon. Take away from me the noise of your songs; to the melody of your harps I will not listen. But let justice roll down like waters, and righteousness like an ever-flowing stream." (Amos 5:21–24)*

An offering or a gift that was given to Yahweh without a heart predisposed to righteousness was analogous to insulting or blaspheming His dignity. In Hebrew, the word 'righteousness' carries other meanings such as justice and inner purity, and it was these qualities that Yahweh expected to accompany the gifts which people presented to Him. Gifts that were given without being accompanied by inner communal or individual predisposition were thus regarded by the Jewish prophets as insulting or degrading to the dignity of Yahweh, who was believed to know the inner secrets hidden in people's hearts. The predominant belief in Judaism is that Yahweh could not be bribed with gifts or sacrifices because He knew the inner predisposition of a human being more than the human being knew about himself. Here it can be said that gifts given as bribery can be difficult to detect, which demonstrates our human fallibility when it comes to understanding the motive behind given gifts.

In traditional African religious thought, purity of heart similarly played a critical role in whether a gift or sacrifice was to be accepted by the ancestors. A gift or sacrifice for the ancestors served two roles. Firstly, it helped to strengthen communion between the community of the living and the ancestors. The communion that exists between the living and their ancestors is well-articulated by the African traditional doctor, Vusamazulu Credo Mutwa:

> *"In the after-death state, an ena, like a physical person, needs nourishment—and this is derived from the prayers and sacrifices of the living. A sacrificed animal's ena goes to feed the ena of the ancestor in whose honor and sacrifice has been conducted. Even the thoughts of the living, we believe, can sustain the enas of our ancestors; that is why people who do what is called 'ancestor worship' are very serious about remembering and propitiating the enas of their ancestors…"* (Mutwa 1996:19–20)

Secondly, a sacrifice that is offered in honour of the ancestors helps the community of the living to remember their existence. A gift in this regard is a symbolic expression of the symbiotic relationship that exists between the living community and the ancestors. This relationship can be severed when there is discord between the ancestors in the world of immortality and their descendants in the realm of mortality. It can only be sustained when the harmony that exists between the ancestors in the realm of immortality is actualised in social harmony and tranquillity. For example, harmony and tranquillity is regarded as the greatest good that is cherished by the ancestors. The same idea was expressed by Michael Gelfand in his anthropological study of the Shona people's ethic of 'relationality' or *ukama* in which he said:

> *"The family spirit or* mudzimu *[ancestral spirit] wants peace amongst the brothers in the family and this cannot exist if there is inequality amongst them. Therefore, it is basic to good living to share with and help one another. In this way jealousy between members of the family is greatly lessened. Thus,* mudzimu *would not approve of one brother acquiring a large amount of material comforts whilst another life in comparative poverty."* (Gelfand 1981:9)

Here again, one finds the same motif of righteousness implied as a necessary precondition for a harmonious relationship between the realm of mortality and immortality.

The second function of a gift is based on the acknowledgement by the living that all material things have their origins in the realm of immortality and when given, should be received with an acknowledgement of its divine origins. Ancestors or *mudzimu* expect their gifts to be reciprocated by righteousness in the lives of their progenitors. The ancestors reciprocate the righteousness of their progenitors by sending rains, ensuring that the soil is fertile and protecting people against epidemics (Gelfand 1981:9). When a bumper harvest was received, it was expected that it had to be reciprocated with a show of gratitude to the ancestors through a thanksgiving ceremony. An attitude of gratitude was thus regarded as an utmost expression of being a well-mannered or well-cultured person.

In contemporary times, the idea of gift-giving manifests as bribery, in the sense that the giver is understood to be expecting some favour in the near future. The rationale of neoliberal capitalism does not give room for the existence of 'free gifts' and African culture is similarly not immune to this idea. Gifts are seen as part and parcel of the rationale of neoliberal capitalistic utility maximization motives. But is there a cultural understanding of gifts that has nothing to do with the motive of economic gain for utility maximization purposes? From my own childhood, I can recall memories of my maternal grandmother visiting us and bringing a 10kg bag full of indigenous *mashuku* fruits, a delicious fruit that did not grow in my native village. Although we enjoyed eating these delicious indigenous fruits, it was not the sole reason we enjoyed our grandmother's visits; her sheer presence brought us great joy. All of her grandchildren competed for her attention and when it was time for her to return home, it was our greatest pleasure to see her being given a bag full of assorted gifts from our parents. In this example, it can be deduced that the gift of *mashuku* fruits was motivated by feelings of love and could not be said to stem from a purely economic incentive. A feeling that overwhelmed all of us was the sense that we were very important to her, and it was for this reason that we longed for her to stay with us.

Corruption and Neoliberal Capitalism

The logic of neoliberal capitalism is conducive to the flourishing of corruption in organisations, companies and other social institutions. However, as we have seen previously, various Western liberal economists and philosophers have claimed that human nature inherently inclines towards evil and corruption; in fact, they considered such vices necessary for economic prosperity. In neoliberal capitalism, utility maximization is regarded as the ultimate goal for economic activities, with the means used to achieve it being of little consequence.

In the context of post-colonial Africa, corrupt governments have attracted many investments from transnational companies compared to countries that have zero-tolerance policies towards corruption. When multinational companies are sometimes found guilty of involvement in corrupt activities, the incident is frequently dubbed a 'scandal' rather than associated with 'corruption'. The bigger the company is, the more immune it becomes to being considered corrupt. William Saunderson-Meyer made a similar observation when he said, "The world's mega-business entities have considerable advantages when compared with their smaller counterparts. Their wealth, their cross-border operations, their ability to collude against market entrants, to influence politicians, to intimidate critics, and—when all else fails—to suborn law enforcement and judicial officials, make them pretty much immune to control."

In other words, the economic power of large multinational companies makes them immune to all sorts of societal prohibitions and exempt from punishment. Their power is beyond reproach from the laws of any nation-states. Saunderson-Meyer sums this up: "Some have more real power than many national states. It makes for arrogance, an imperviousness to criticism, and an indifference to ethical conventions. So when, once in a blue moon, one these giants is brought to its knees, there is a certain schandenfreude. Everyone enjoys seeing the bully taking a well-deserved, long-delayed 'thumping.'" (Saunderson-Meyer 2017:3)

Economic power that results from amassing enormous amounts of wealth creates a situation in which multinational companies amass power that surpasses that of the nation-state. In fact, with such a vast amount of wealth at their disposal, these companies are known to influence state policy and even play a prominent role in the formation of governments and executives. The participation of multinational companies in governments undoubtedly makes them a law unto themselves.

Other scholars such as William De Maria have argued that there is no consensus among Western scholars on whether corruption is beneficial or detrimental to the economy. De Maria argues against the popular orthodox view of corruption by using statistical data to show that countries which score higher on corruption levels have a higher GDP than those with lower scores. He writes, "The high-corruption countries have growth rates far higher than the low-corruption countries. Notwithstanding an active dissension in the literature, Western-based certainties about the nature of corruption prevail. The irony is that this certainty has failed to yield any worthwhile measures of the phenomenon" (De Maria 2009:364). It is evident that De Maria is debunking the notion that corruption is detrimental to economic growth, as it is in fact the reason for higher growth rates in countries that are infested with corruption. For De Maria, the corruption mantra serves the economic interests of Western countries that are mainly promoted by the International Monetary Fund and the World Bank. In post-colonial Africa, greed that usually manifests itself through corruption has resulted in the collapse of public institutions, and in some cases, has been given ample opportunity to thrive through the end of the rule of law and politics.

References

Adedeji, A. 1982. "Development and Economic Growth in Africa to the Year 200: Alternative Projections and Policies", in Shaw, T. (ed.), *Alternative Futures for Africa*. pp. 279–304.

Ake, C. 1981. "Historical and Theoretical Background: The Political Context of Indigenisation", in Adedeji, A. (ed.), *Indigenisation of African Economies*. London: Hutchinson University Library for Africa.

Ayittey, G. 1998. *Africa in Chaos*. New York: St Martin's Press.

Axelrod, R. 1984. *The Evolution of Co-operation*. Middlesex: Penguin Books Ltd.

Bigongiari I. D. (ed.) 1973. *The Political Ideas of St. Thomas Aquinas*. New York: Hafiner Press.

Black Economic Commission. 2001. *Black Commission Economic Commission Report*. Johannesburg: Skotaville Press.

Beets S. D. 2007. "Global Corruption and Religion: An Empirical Examination", in *Journal of Global Ethics*, Vol. 3, No. 1, April, pp. 69–85.

Boulaga F. B. 1984. *Christianity without Fetishes: An African Critique of Christianity*. Lit verlag: Hamburg.

Bujo, B. 1997. *The Ethical Dimension of Community: The African Model and the Dialogue Between North and South*. Nairobi: Pauline Publications Africa.

Bujo, B. 1998. *The Ethical Dimension of Community: The African Model and the Dialogue between North and South*. Nairobi: Pauline Publications Africa.

Byrne, P. 1989. *Natural Religion and the Nature of Religion: The Legacy of Deism*. London: Routledge.

Comaroff, J. L. and Comaroff, J. 2009. *Ethnicity, Inc*. Scottsville: University of KwaZulu-Natal Press.

Canterbery , E. R. 1987. *The Making of Economics*. Belmont: Wadsworth.

Chan, W. 1963. *Instructions*. Graham, A.C. 1923. (trans.) London: Lund Humphries.

Chinweizu, I. 1999. "Africa and the Capitalist Countries", in Mazrui, A. A. and Wondji, C. (eds.), *General History of Africa VIII: Africa since 1935* (Unabridged Edition). London: James Currey.

Chisala C. "Indigenisation of Privatization (Part 2): Some General Comments on Privatization and Capitalism", file://E:\Indigenisation%200f%20Privatisation –Botswana.htm, Accessed 22 April 2007)

Cort, J. C. 1988. *Christian Socialism: An Informal History*. New York: Orbis Books.

Daly, H. and Cobb, J. B. Jr. 1989. *For the Common Good: Redirecting the Economy Toward Community, the Environment and a Sustainable Future*. Boston: Beacon Press.

Darwin, C. 1859. *On the Origins of Species by Means of Natural Selection*. London: Murray.

Davis, H. R. 1973. "Interpreting the Colonial Period in African History", in *African Affairs*, vol. 72 no. 289, 383–400.

Dawkins, R. 1976. *The Selfish Gene*. Oxford: Oxford University Press.

Deklerk, W. A. 1975. *The Puritans in Africa: A Story of Afrikanerdom*. New York: Pelican.

De Maria, W. 2009. "Does African 'Corruption' Exist?" in Murove, M. F. (ed.), *African Ethics: An Anthology of Comparative and Applied Ethics*. Scottsville: University of KwaZulu-Natal Press, pp.357–374.

De Soto, H. 2000. *The Mystery of Capital: Why Capitalism Triumphs in the West and Fails Everywhere Else*. London: Bantam.

Gadir, A. A. 1994. "Donors' Wisdom versus African Folly: What Academic Freedom and which High Moral Standing?" in Mamdani, M. and Diouf, M. (eds.) *Academic Freedom in Africa*. Dakar: CODESRIA, pp. 109–117.

Gelfand M. 1981. *Ukama: Reflections on Shona and Western Cultures in Zimbabwe*. Gweru: Mambo Press.

Giliomee, H. 1983. "The Afrikaner Economic Advance", in Adam, H. and Giliomee, H. *The Rise and Crisis of AFRIKANER POWER*. Cape Town: David Philip.

Gonzalez, J. L. 1990. *Faith and Wealth: A History of Early Christian Ideas on the Origin and Significance and Use of Money*. New York: Harper Collins.

Gross, F. 1956. *Rhodes of Africa*. London: Cassell.

Hamlin, A. P. 1986. *Ethics, Economics and the State*. Sussex: Wheatsheaf Books Ltd.

Hamutyinei, M. A. and Plangger, A. 1987. *Tsumo-Shumo: Shona Proverbial Wisdom and Lore*. Gweru: Mambo Press.

Hanna, A. J. 1961. *European Rule in Africa*. London: Routledge.

Hayek, F. A. 1948. *Individualism and Economic Order*. Chicago: University of Chicago Press.

Heilbroner, R. L. 1972a. *The Worldly Philosophers: The Lives, Times and Ideas of the Great Economic Thinkers*. New York: Simon and Schuster.

Heilbroner, R. L. 1972b. *The Nature and Logic of Capitalism*. London: Norton and Company.

Heyne, P. 1983. *The Economic Way of Thinking*. Washington: Science and Research Associates.

Hill, C. 1958. *Puritanism and Revolution: Studies in Interpretation of the English Revolution of the 17th Century*. London: Secker & Warburg.

Hirschman, A. 1977. *The Passions and the Interests: Political Arguments for Capitalism Before its Triumph*. Princeton: Princeton University Press.

Hobbes, T. 1962. *Leviathan: Or the Matter, Forme and Power of a Commonwealth Ecclesiastical and Civil*. Oakeshott, M. (ed.). Collier-Macmillan Ltd: London.

Hume, D. 1882. *A Treatise of Human Nature*. Nidditch, P. (ed.). 1978. Oxford: Oxford University Press.

Hunter, G. 1967. *The Best of Both Worlds? A Challenge on Development Policies in Africa*. London: Oxford University Press.

Jack, V. Haris, K. 2007. *Broad Based BEE: The Complete Guide*. Northcliff: Frontrunner Publishing (Pty).

Keigwin, H. S. 1923. "Native Development", in *NADA – The Southern Rhodesia Native Development Annual*, No. 1. 2/6 December, pp. 10–17.

Kennedy, P. 1988. *African Capitalism: The Struggle for Ascendancy*. Cambridge: Cambridge University Press.

Kenyatta, J. 1953. *Facing Mount Kenya*. London: Secker and Warburg.

Knight, C. 1991. *Blood Relations: Menstruation and the Origins of Culture*. London: Yale University Press.

Komter A. E. 2005. *Social Solidarity and the Gift*. Cambridge: Cambridge University Press.

Laue, von, T. H. 1987. *The World Revolution of Westernisation: The Twentieth Century in Global Perspective*. Oxford: Oxford University Press.

Lenin, V. I. 1947. *Imperialism: The Highest Stage of Capitalism*. Moscow: Foreign Languages Publishing House.

Lipton, M. 1986. *Capitalism and Apartheid South Africa, 1910–1986*. Cape Town: David Philip, Publisher (PTY) LTD.

Luther, M. 1962. *The Christian in Society*. II, Vol. 45. Brandt, W. and Lehmann, H. eds. Philadelphia: Fortress Press.

Machiavelli, N. 1961. *The Prince*. Bull, G. (trans). Suffolk: The Chaucer Press.

Mafeje, A. 1971. "The Ideology of Tribalism", in *The Journal of Modern African Studies*. Vol. 9, No.2, pp. 253–261.

Magee, S. P. 2000. "Bioeconomics: Lessons for Business, Nations and Life", in Colander, D. (ed.). *The Complexity Vision and the Teaching of Economics*. Cheltenham: Edward Edgar Publishing Limited, pp. 255–284.

Malthus, T. R. 1958. *An Essay on the Principle of Population as It Affects the Future Improvement of Society*. London: John Murray.

Mandeville, B. de. 1924. *The Fable of the Bees*. Vol. 2. Kaye, F. B. (ed.). Oxford: Oxford University Press.

Margolis, H. 1982. *Selfishness, Altruism, and Rationality*. Cambridge: Cambridge University Press.

Martin, D. and Johnson, P. 1981. *The Struggle for Zimbabwe*. Johannesburg: Ravan Press.

Marx, K. and Engels, F. 1975. *Karl Marx and Frederick Engels: Collected Works*. Vol. 3. Cohen, J. et al. (eds.) Moscow: Progress Publishers.

Mauss, M. 1990. *The Gift: The Form and Reason for exchange in Archaic Societies*. London: Routledge.

Mazrui, A. A. 1983. "Political Engineering in Africa", in *The International Social Science Journal*. Vol. XXV, No. 2. UNESCO, pp. 279–294.

Mazrui, A. A. 1986. *The Africans: A Triple Heritage*. London: BBC Publications.

Mazrui, A. A. 1990. *Cultural Forces in World Politics*. London: James Currey.

Mazrui, A. A. 1994. "The Impact of Global Changes on Academic Freedom in Africa: A Preliminary Assessment", in Mamdani, M. and Diouf, M. (eds.), *Academic Freedom in Africa*. Dakar: CODESRIA, pp. 118–138.

Mazrui, A. A. 1999. "Trends in Philosophy and Science in Africa", in Mazrui, A.A. and Wondji, C. (eds.), *General History of Africa VIII: Africa Since 1935*. Oxford: James Currey Ltd. pp. 633–677.

Mbaku, J. M. 2000. *Bureaucratic and Political Corruption in Africa: The Public Choice Perspective*. Florida: Krieger Publishing Company.

Mbiti, J. 1976. *African Religions and Philosophy*. London: Heinemann.

Meredith, M. 1979. *The Past is Another Country: Rhodesia, 1890–1979*. London: Andre Deutsch.

Meredith, M. 2005. *The State of Africa: A History of Fifty Years of Independence*. Johannesburg: Jonathan Ball Publishers.

Mudenge, S. I .G. 1988. *A Political History of Munhumutapa, c 1400–1902*. London: James Currey Publishers.

Murove, M. F. 1999. "The Shona Concept of Ukama and the Process Philosophical Concept of Relatedness, with Special Reference to the Ethical Implications of the Contemporary Neo-Liberal Economic Practices". Pietermaritzburg: University of Natal (Unpublished MA Thesis).

Murove, M. 2008. "Moving Beyond Dehumanisation and Greed in the Light of African Economic Ethics: A Statement", in *Religion & Theology* (15), 74–76.

Mutwa, V. C. 1996. *Songs of the Stars: The Lore of a Zulu Shaman*. Larsen S. (ed.), New York: Barrtown.

Nill, M. 1985. *Morality and Self-Interest in Protagoras, Antiphon and Democritus*. Leiden: Brill.

Nkrumah, K. 1970. *Africa Must Unite*. London: Panaf Books Ltd.

Nyerere, J. K. 1968. *Freedom and Socialism: Uhuru na Ujamaa*. Oxford: Oxford University Press.

Polanyi, K. 1968. *The Great Transformation: The Political and Economic Origins of our Time*. New York: Renehart and Company, Inc.

Radebe, P. 2007. "Managing the Labyrinth" in *Mail & Guardian*. Available at: https://mg.co.za/article/2007-04-23-managing-the-labyrinth.

Ranger, T. O. 1993. "The Invention of Tradition in Colonial Africa", in Hobsbawn, E. and Ranger, T.O. (eds.) in *The Invention of Tradition*. New York: Cambridge University Press.

Robertson, A. F. 2001. *Greed: Gut Feelings, Growth, and History*. Oxford: Blackwell Publishers Ltd.

Rorty, A. O. (Ed.) 2001. *The Many Faces of Evil: Historical Perspectives*. London: London and New York.

Ruskin, J. 1862. *Unto this Last: Four Essays on the First Principle of Political Economy*. London: W. H. Allen.

Saunderson-Meyer, W. "Supposedly too big to fail: Certainly too Slippery to Police", Available at: https://www.biznews.com/global-citizen/2017/10/16/kpmg-mcknsey-arent-too-big-to-fail (Accessed 10 November 2017).

Schumpeter, J. 1986. *History of Economic Analysis*. New York: Oxford University Press.

Sen, A. 1987. *On Ethics and Economics*. Oxford: Basil Blackwell Ltd.

Shewring, W. 1948. *Rich and Poor in Christian Tradition*. London: Burns and Oates.

Singer, P. 1995. *How Are We to Live? Ethics in an Age of Self-Interest*. New York: Prometheus Books.

Sithole, M. 1985. "The Salience of Ethnicity in African Politics: The Case of Zimbabwe", in *Journal of Asian and African Studies*. XX, 3–4, pp. 181–192.

Smith, A. 1872. *The Theory of Moral Sentiments*. London: Murray &Co.

Smith, A. 1976. A*n Inquiry into the Nature and Causes of the Wealth of Nations*. Campbell, R. H., Skinner, A. S. and Todd, W. B. (eds.). New York: Modern Library.

Spencer, H. 1907. *The Data of Ethics*. London: William & Norgate.

Tawney, R. H. 1926. *Religion and the Rise of Capitalism: A Historical Study*. Harmondsworth: Penguin Books Ltd.

Radcliffe, T. 1994. "Jurassic Park or Last Supper", in *The Tablet*, pp. 761–763.

Troeltsch, E. 1931. *The Social Teaching of the Christian Churches*. Vol. I. Wyon, O. (Trans.). London: George Allen & Unwin Ltd.

Tullock, G. and Mackenzie, R. 1985. *The New World of Economics: Explorations into the Human Existence*. Homewood: Richard D. Irwin, Inc.

Van Onselen, C. 1976. *Chibaro: African Mine Labour in Southern Rhodesia 1900–1933*. London: Pluto Press.

Vaux, K. L. 1992. *Ethics and the Gulf War: Religion, Rhetoric and Righteousness*. Boulder: Westview Press.

Veblen, T. 1931. *The Theory of the Leisure Class: An Economic Study of Institutions*. New York: The Modern Library.

Viner, J. 1958. *The Long View and the Short: Studies in Economic Theory and Policy*. Illinois: The Free Press.

Viner, J. 1978. *Religious Thought and Economic Society*. Melitz, J. and Winch, D. (eds.). Durham: Duke University Press.

Weber, M. 1958. *The Protestant Ethic and the Spirit of Capitalism*. London: Allen and Unwin.

Wicksteed, P. H. 1946. *The Common Sense of Political Economy and Selected Papers and Reviews on Economic Theory*. London: Routledge.

Wilson, N. H. 1923. "The Development of Native Reserves", in *Southern Rhodesia Native Affairs Department Annual* (NADA). Vol. II, pp. 86–96.

Xenos, N. 1989. *Scarcity & Modernity*. Routledge: London and New York.

Zondi, N. S. T. 2012. "Tenders and Corruption in post-apartheid South Africa: Rethinking African Ethics as a Panacea for Corruption", University of KwaZulu-Natal, [Unpublished MA Thesis].

Index

A

Adedeji, Adebayo 104, 122
African Growth Opportunity Act (AGOA) 57
Africanization 104, 107, 113–122
Afrikaner Broederbond 26
Afrobarometer Survey 139
Ake, Claude 106, 115–117
almsgiving 5
America 7, 8, 15, 17, 21, 39, 43–51, 56–58, 97, 99, 129, 131, 132
apartheid 21, 24–30, 33, 34, 38, 103, 104, 108, 110, 113, 119, 120, 145
  post-apartheid 20, 36, 103, 126
Aquinas, St. Thomas 5, 6
Augustine of Hippo, St. 4, 5
Axelrod, Robert 81

B

Belgium 13, 16, 100
Berlin Conference 34
Black Economic Empowerment (BEE) 103–109, 113–127, 136, 153, 154
British Empire 18, 55, 56
Bush, President George W. 44, 132

C

Cape Colony 26

Cape Town 25
capitalism
  advent of 8, 19, 31, 92, 145
  booty 14, 15, 19, 39–44
  colonial i, 8, 12–15, 19, 31, 32, 99, 103, 104, 113, 117, 126, 133, 135, 145
  failure of 130, 131
  modern i, 1–9, 12, 15, 18, 31, 55, 62, 88, 91, 92, 96, 97, 109
  political i, 12, 109, 119, 121, 124–127, 130–134, 137
  spirit of 6, 7
  transmission of 32
Chisala, Chanda 107, 164
Christianity
  Church Fathers 3–6, 61, 143
  evangelization 3, 16, 17
  Protestant ethic 2, 3, 8–11, 14, 97. *See also* Max Weber
  reformed Protestantism 6, 7
Clinton, Bill 57
colonialism i, 1–3, 8, 9, 12, 13, 17, 18, 26, 29–39, 42, 54, 97, 100–103,
    109–113, 119, 120, 123, 125, 129, 130, 136, 142, 145
  decolonisation 106, 113, 114, 116
  neo-colonialism 38, 39
Comaroff, Jean and John 133–136
Congo 13, 16, 17, 43, 100, 133

D

Darwin, Charles 75–77
Dawkins, Richard 77
Deism 68
Democritus 60, 61

E

economic growth 37, 57, 111, 142, 161
economic nationalism 12, 26, 30, 111, 112, 118
Engels, Friedrich 71, 77
Ethics and Anti-Corruption Commission 141
ethnic identity 37, 134, 135. *See also* tribalism
Europe 1, 7, 8, 17, 18, 100, 112, 129
euthymia 60
evolution 75, 78, 131, 136

F

foreign aid 39–42, 48–50

G

Gaddafi, Muammar 45, 46
game theory of cooperation 81
gift-giving 154, 155, 159
globalisation 47, 102
Gossen, Heinrich 8
greed
  in biology 77
  in traditional African societies 10, 32, 91, 145. *See also* prestige motive
  psychology of 29, 72

H

Hancock, Graham 49–51
Harvey, David 44
Hayek, Friedrich von 69, 70
Hebrew 157
Hobbes, Thomas 85, 86
Hobson, A. J. 52–55
Hume, David 63, 87, 88
Hussein, Saddam 44, 45

I

imperialism i, 13–17, 29–32, 38, 39, 44, 47, 48, 51–58, 97, 106, 107, 113, 117
indigenization 12, 103–108, 113–125, 136
Institutional Evolutionary Economics 106, 115
International Monetary Fund (IMF) 39, 42, 47, 49, 57, 58, 101
invisible hand 67–70
Israel 27, 156

J

Johnson, President Lyndon Baines 56

K

Kenya 41, 126, 140, 141

L

laissez-faire 67
Land Apportionment Act 19
Latin America 47, 49
Lenin, Vladimir 15, 52
Leopold II, King 13, 16, 17
Leverhulme, Lord William 52
Libya 45, 46
Luther, Martin 6, 62

M

Machiavelli, Niccole 84, 85
Malthus, Thomas 76, 77
Mandeville, Bernard de 64–67, 144, 154
Manuel, Trevor 104
Marx, Karl 71, 77
Moyo, Dambisa 41
multinational companies 123, 125, 140, 160, 161

N

National Environmental Management Agency (NEMA) 141
Native Affairs Commission 22
Native Reserves 19, 33–36, 136
Natives Land Act 21–26
natural selection 75–78
neoliberalism 4, 47, 57, 58, 69, 73, 79, 101, 102, 115, 131, 134, 159, 160
nepotism 37, 140–143, 147
Nigeria 100, 124, 125
Nkrumah, Kwame 38–40, 52, 110, 114, 115
no-fly zone 46
Nyerere, Julius 111, 112
Nzimande, Blade 125, 126

O

Oil-for-Food Programme (OIP) 45

P

Perkins, John 40–42
Platinum Belt 36
Polanyi, Karl 92, 93
population geography 76
prestige motive 10, 11, 97, 98, 146–151
profit motive 32, 97, 124
Providence 4, 27, 68, 69. *See also* Christianity

R

regional economic communities (RECs) 128
Rhodes, Cecil John 18, 19, 55, 109
Rhodesia 18, 19, 33, 34, 55, 93, 135
Ruskin, John 70

S

Seko, Mobuto Sese 100
self-interest 8, 56, 62, 66, 67, 70, 78, 80, 81, 85, 88, 95, 96, 143, 154
Shona 19, 32, 91, 94, 95, 105, 146, 151–153, 158
Sierra Leone 100
Smith, Adam 64, 67–69, 77
socialism 112, 145
Southern African Development Community (SADC) 128
specialization 74, 116
Spencer, Herbert 73
Stevens, President Siaka 100
Structural Adjustment Programs (ESAP) 57

T

tax xi, 12, 17, 93, 109, 140, 142, 150
tenders 108, 109, 120–126, 136, 142, 153
theory of the leisure class 153. *See also* Thorstein Veblen
Tilden, Samuel 69
Transparency International 139, 151
Transvaal 18, 25
tribalism 33–37, 140, 152, 153
Tribal Trust land 36
Trump, President Donald 56

U

ubuntu 136, 145, 147
United Nations (UN) 45, 50, 51, 56, 57
  UNECA 140
  UNSC 46, 56
utility maximization 80–82, 159, 160

V

Veblen, Thorstein 71–73, 105, 106, 115–117, 153, 154
Verwoed, Hendricks 110

W

war
  Gulf War 44, 45
  Middle East conflict 47
  Second World War 29
Weber, Max 2, 3, 7–10, 14, 15, 19
welfarism 77
Wicksteed, Philip 82, 83, 144
World Bank 39, 42, 47, 49, 56–58, 101, 161

X

Xun Zi 85

Z

Zimbabwe i, 18–20, 91, 121, 151
Zulu 25, 32, 90, 153

www.ingramcontent.com/pod-product-compliance
Lightning Source LLC
Chambersburg PA
CBHW031511270326
41930CB00006B/350